Acknowledgements

We have appreciated the opportunity to work in hundreds of school districts throughout the country for many years. As we have shared our work with many educators and parents, they shared back, telling us what does and doesn't work, what is and isn't a priority and why. So to the thousands of educators who go about their work quietly and diligently, striving to make a difference in the lives of young people, we offer our heartfelt thanks. Many of the principles and qualities which educators and parents use for the mutual benefit of our children have become a significant part of the *Parents on Board* program. Your work, your voice and your dedication continue to energize this program for parents and schools.

We also appreciate the dedicated and gifted work of the product development department at Active Parenting Publishers. Specifically, Suzanne De Galan for her excellent product management and editorial work; Lisa Wasshausen for ensuring on-time and high quality production of video and print materials; Jim Polak for another fine design effort, with assistance from designer Rick Raschke; Nancy Ballance and Michele Cox for their able research assistance; and Kelli Phillips for doing a great job typing scripts and manuscripts.

Thank you also to Video Producer Genie Wood, Director Mike Speltz and the rest of the Avid video staff whose combined efforts brought the characters to life with a quality video production.

We also acknowledge the dedicated educators who served on the advisory board for this project: Joe Finley, Principal, Marietta, Ohio; Mary Gerke, President of the American School Counselor Association and Counselor, Racine, Wisconsin; Caroline B. Hecht, Coordinator of Volunteer Services, Atlanta, Georgia; Martha Kotun, Kindergarten Teacher, Trumansburg, New York; Darryl Yagi, Counselor, Petaluma, California.

To these and all the others whose encouragement, knowledge and goodwill helped in the development of this program, we are sincerely grateful.

Michael H. Popkin, Ph.D.
Bettie B. Youngs, Ph.D., Ed.D.
Jane M. Healy, Ph.D.

Photography by Ben Smith

Table of Contents

The research results are overwhelming. Your active involvement in your children's education is the single most important factor in their academic success. It is more important than who your children's teachers are. It is more important than the quality of the materials and facilities at your children's school. It is even more important than your own education or economic level.

An impressive body of research compiled over the last two decades shows clearly that children whose parents are involved in their education:

- get better grades and test scores.

- do more homework.

- have better attendance.

- have higher graduation rates.

- are more likely to go on to college or other postsecondary education.

- are more involved in extracurricular activities.

- demonstrate a more positive attitude and better behavior all around.

In addition, children whose parents are more involved in their learning are less likely to have behavior or academic problems, to repeat a grade or to be suspended or expelled.

Parent involvement looks different in every home, but one thing remains constant: Parents who are involved see themselves as partners in their children's education. They are on board with the goals of the school, and they work to see that their children achieve these goals. With such a powerful partnership supporting them, children do better in school and in life.

The purpose of the *Parents on Board* program is to give you specific ways to be positively involved in your children's education. Even if you are already involved, this program will show you how to build on your efforts to support your children and your children's school.

In the *Parents on Board* program, you will learn about proven methods for helping your children succeed in school, such as:

- developing a structured but not rigid home environment that promotes learning.

- having high but realistic expectations for your children's success.

- encouraging curiosity, problem solving and independent thinking in your children.

- encouraging positive behavior in your children.

■ modeling lifelong learning and the value of education.

■ building positive parent-teacher relationships.

■ supporting the discipline policy of your children's school.

■ understanding your children's learning styles and how to develop and strengthen them.

■ becoming "positive coaches" when helping your children with school work.

■ encouraging language development through reading, talking and listening.

■ making learning part of everyday life.

The information and skills you'll learn here will not only help your children do better in school, they will also help your children's school be more effective in helping your children. As Dr. James Hendrix of the Lovett School in Atlanta stated, "The difference between a good school and a great school is the support and involvement of parents." Your participation is that powerful. And as you increase your involvement in your children's education, you may also find your own educational journey invigorated in new ways. Welcome on board!

Session 1

PREPARING YOUR CHILD TO SUCCEED

Chapter 1

All parents want their children to succeed, but they're not always sure how to help. Even bright youngsters may struggle in school, and many families undergo needless arguments and frustration in their effort to make a difference. These families may be smart, but they're not "school-smart."

In school-smart families, parents know how to support their children effectively in academic tasks. They communicate firm and realistic standards and set up a home climate that contributes to positive achievement. They use cooperative strategies to help teachers help their children learn. School-smart families realize there are different kinds of intelligence and learning styles, and that children of many different abilities can develop into successful and confident adults. In fact, we now know that attitudes and motivation are often much more important in the long run than "brains."

Whether your child is an excellent student or a more reluctant learner, your involvement is important. Your support, encouragement and help can spell the difference between frustration and success, between a "turned-off, tuned-out" child and an enthusiastic learner who finds school interesting, meaningful and a source of excitement. Volumes of research demonstrate clearly:

■ Children whose parents value academic success do better in school—and in life.

■ Children whose parents devote time and energy to support their learning tend to have higher levels of motivation and fewer academic, behavioral or emotional problems.

By reading this book, you have demonstrated how important your child's school success is to you. You may be eager to jump right into academics, to what you see as the core of school success, and learn immediately how to help your child read at a higher level, compute more difficult sums and strengthen spelling skills. But learning is more than the "three r's." Before tackling specific academic disciplines, you should know something about your child's individual learning styles and habits and be able to assess his basic learning readiness.

Educators and psychologists are currently placing much less emphasis on the thing called "intelligence" (IQ) than they did even five years ago. In fact, knowing about your child's inherited "smarts" is less important for understanding or predicting academic achievement than other factors:

■ your child's particular "learning style"

■ your child's "learning habits"

Learning Styles

Not every child learns in the same way. If you have more than one child, you may have already noticed differences in your children's learning styles. Perhaps your son readily learns anything that is set to music, while your daughter remembers things she sees better than things she hears. Aspects of a child's "learning style" may show up in subtle ways:

■ Some people prefer to study in the morning, others at night.

■ Some people enjoy reading while sitting at a desk, others may prefer to read curled up on the floor or lying down in bed.

■ Some people like brightly lighted rooms, others prefer dimmer lights.

■ Some people can tolerate background noise, others cannot.

■ Some people prefer to learn by listening, some by looking, others by writing down and others by using a combination. Preferences may also vary according to the type of material being learned.

Seven Types of Intelligence

According to Harvard psychologist Howard Gardner, there are at least seven types of intelligence which are combined in varying degrees in all of us. These are:

1. Linguistic
2. Logical or Mathematical
3. Musical
4. Spatial or Visual
5. Kinesthetic
6. Interpersonal
7. Intrapersonal

Let's take a closer look at each one.

1. **Linguistic Intelligence.** This is our ability to read and write, to use words well. Writers, speakers and politicians are strong in

linguistic intelligence. Children who are linguistically intelligent may also be systematic, enjoying sequential patterns and order. They have good memories for what they read and hear and they enjoy word games. Linguistic intelligence is highly prized in our school system. Teachers often use stories, vocabulary games and discussions to teach material. Students who have not developed their linguistic intelligence may have difficulty learning by using these techniques. They may feel confused and not capable.

2. **Logical or Mathematical Intelligence.** This ability, most often developed in scientists, mathematicians and lawyers, is the ability to reason or calculate. Children who have well-developed logical intelligence like to analyze, to understand what causes things to happen. They are often good at using computers and understanding the orderly nature of programming and application. They enjoy problem solving. Schools also reward people with logical or mathematical intelligence. Deductive thinking is emphasized in the classroom. Students who do not have this type of logical intelligence quickly feel left out.

3. **Musical Intelligence.** Musically intelligent people are very sensitive to the emotional power of music and aware of its complex organization. Cultures without written languages that use music to communicate place a high value on musical intelligence. In our society, however, we do not often classify musical ability as intelligence, but dismiss it lightly as a "knack" or a "gift." Children who have musical intelligence can reduce the stress of learning by integrating music with other subject areas. They can learn dates and other "have-to-memorize" material through rap or other forms of rhythm. Perhaps more importantly, children with musical intelligence can use music to help them relax and change their moods.

4. **Spatial or Visual Intelligence.** Architects, sculptors and pilots test high in this area. A battlefield strategist needs to be highly spatially intelligent. Children with this intelligence can remember things well when they are put into picture form. They use mental images and metaphors for learning. They may be good at memorizing maps and charts. Unfortunately, our schools often present material sequentially, only gradually working up to conclusions. This practice can frustrate the spatially gifted child, who wants to see the whole first, then come back to flesh out the details.

5. **Kinesthetic Intelligence.** Also called physical intelligence, this type is highly developed in athletes, dancers, gymnasts and surgeons. Kinesthetically intelligent children have good control over their bodies and like to use them in sports, dance—anything that requires coordination and movement. They have good timing and are highly sensitive to the physical environment. These children learn best by doing, by touching, by moving objects around; they enjoy models and handicrafts. Such children become stressed when they are forced to sit still for too long, when they must listen but not participate physically.

6. **Interpersonal Intelligence.** "People people," or those who relate well to others, score high in interpersonal intelligence. Salespeople, negotiators, motivational speakers and coaches have high interpersonal intelligence. Children with this intelligence are very social. They tend to join groups, understand other children, communicate—even manipulate—quite well. They may enjoy school activities that require partners or teamwork better than situations demanding solo activity. These children need to take breaks from work in order to socialize and to keep in touch with other students.

7. **Intrapersonal Intelligence.** Often called intuition, intrapersonal intelligence is the ability to tap into information stored in the subconscious mind. Philosophers and counselors show this type of intelligence. Children who have intrapersonal intelligence are very sensitive. They understand themselves well and are self-motivated. They do not do well when teachers spell out every detail of a project or insist that something be done by the book. Intrapersonal people want to be different; they want to use their self-knowledge and to develop their own feelings. They like to have a purpose in life and are aware of their own strengths and weaknesses. In the classroom, these students often become upset when expected to conform. They usually learn more quickly when they are allowed to do independent study activities and to take control of their own learning.

Different Kids/Different Styles

All children have more than one kind of intelligence; in fact, most children will wield strength in two or three areas. Observe each of your children. Even though we believe that learning style is at least partially inherited, it is very likely that "gifts" or "strengths"—those one or two areas in which the child finds mastery relatively easy—will be very different for each child. If your child's talents are different from yours—such as a gifted mechanic in a family of lawyers—it's foolish to try to force choices against his natural inclinations. The last thing a parent wants is to squelch a natural ability that may blossom into a life's calling by steering a child toward more conventionally valued studies. This is one

If your child's talents are different from yours—such as a gifted mechanic in a family of lawyers—it's foolish to try to force choices against his natural inclinations.

good reason to expose our children to a variety of activities and celebrate their triumphs and skills in every arena of learning and life.

Even children less adept at certain intelligences can improve them if they believe it's worthwhile to try.

While all seven intelligences are important in the working world, there is no doubt that some of these intelligences—linguistic and mathematical, for example—are more valued in school than others. Even if your children's natural abilities lie elsewhere, you can help them strengthen such "traditional" intelligences as linguistic by encouraging their efforts in these areas and using positive coaching (as described in Chapters 6, 7 and 8). Even children less adept at certain intelligences can improve them if they believe it's worthwhile to try. In addition, this book will show you many ways to bolster specific academic skills without forcing them upon your children. Above all, observe and listen to your children—you will learn a lot about the special mix of talents and needs that you can help unfold in each of them. (For more on how people learn, consult the Recommended Reading list.)

Learning Habits

The characteristics of your child's brain are determined partially by genes that your child "got" (inherited) from you. Most of your child's brain development, however, comes as a result of the way he uses his brain after birth. How he plays, wonders, experiments, learns and takes on new mental challenges all form "habits of mind," such as memory and motivation, that will underlie all his learning experiences. Thus the home environment you provide has a lot to do with how well your children will fulfill their natural potential. In order to build your child's ability and readiness to learn, it helps to understand these habits of mind that underlie successful learning. On the next page is a brief description of these basic habits and some guidelines for measuring them in your own children. The remainder of the book will help you develop your children's learning habits and thus strengthen their ability to learn.

Successful Learners:

■ are motivated to learn.

■ are able to focus and pay attention.

■ use language to understand and communicate ideas.

■ use memory to aid learning.

■ solve problems.

■ analyze and adjust their own thinking.

Let's look at each of these skills more closely.

Motivation

This real "basic" of success arises from the multitude of experiences through life that make a child feel powerful as a learner. Does your child believe the following?

■ My efforts make a difference, and I can succeed if I try long enough.

■ It's worth trying even if it's hard, because it makes me feel powerful as a learner, even if I don't succeed on every try.

■ Being smart is not just something you're born with. It depends on the effort you put forth.

Children who believe that working hard makes them smarter are right.

Exciting new research indicates that children who hold these beliefs will be more able to improve their intelligence than those who don't. Children who see intelligence as something you can change through effort, rather than something you either have or don't have, tend to be more highly motivated, get better grades and do better in life. In other words: Children who believe that working hard makes them smarter are right. Everything you will learn in this course will help you help your child develop strong motivation to learn.

Attention

If a child knows how to use his brain's attention mechanisms effectively, all forms of learning come much more easily. Attention span varies according to age, so you should expect it to increase as your child gets older. Here are some questions to consider about your child's attention span:

■ **Can your child stick with a project or task for a reasonable period of time?** Help your child expand attention by limiting distracting activities or noise and by sitting down with her and encouraging her to complete a task. Some children need help planning an activity's steps before they start. Teach them about completing a task by using small steps.

Example

"What do we need to do before we can play that game? Do we need to gather the equipment? What next? Do we know the proper directions? Are we ready to start the game? How will we know when we're finished?"

Children who are allowed some quiet time for independent play learn to manage their own brains better than those who are constantly bombarded with confusion and rushed from activity to activity.

■ **Can your child persist if a task doesn't come easily?** Youngsters of the MTV generation seem to have limited patience, and a "two-minute mind" does not help a child become a good reader or math student. Be sure to limit TV and video games. Expect your child to follow up on household tasks.

Example

"It looks as if half the trash you started to dump is still in the basket, Karen. Will you finish the job, please?"

Chapters 4 and 6 contain sections on stimulating independence in your children and helping them stick with tough jobs.

■ **Can your child shift attention appropriately?** Some youngsters get so engrossed in activities that they can't let go even when they need to. (And they all seem to have difficulty leaving play to set the table!) Teach your child to use attention flexibly by giving some warning before you ask him to do something new.

Example

"In five minutes I'm going to ask you to put the ball away and help set the table."

Exceptional rigidity in behavior, including tantrums when new ideas or activities are introduced, signal a potential learning problem; mention this behavior to your pediatrician.

■ **Do you help your child by providing an organized environment?** A reasonably well-structured household, with appropriate rules and expectations, helps most children develop good attention habits (see Chapter 2 for information on how to increase structure in your family).

Some youngsters have organic problems (e.g., "Attention Deficit Hyperactivity Disorder," or "ADD" or "ADHD") that make it extremely difficult for them to focus appropriately despite the best parental example. A child like this should be seen by a physician or pediatric neurologist to determine treatment. If you suspect your child may have this difficulty, have a heart-to-heart talk with your school counselor or teacher and learn more by consulting suggested books in the Recommended Reading list. Then follow up with a medical diagnosis if necessary.

Using Language Effectively

Most kids know how to talk, but good students also know how to use language effectively to understand and communicate ideas. In Chapters 7 and 8 you will find specific information about developing language skills in your child. In the meantime, how can you tell if your child needs help with language? Can your child:

■ listen and remember what she hears?

■ express an idea with reasonable ease?

■ ask questions to get information?

■ take turns appropriately in conversation?

Obviously, your child's facility will vary with age. However, if your child's capability in the above areas is drastically different from other children of the same age, or if the teacher suggests there may be a problem, consider a professional evaluation from the school's speech/language therapist or from a clinic.

Memory

Memory is a peculiar thing—the quality of our memory usually depends on what we're trying to remember! Some people are good at retaining things they hear, while others focus more on what they see. Some people easily remember how to get somewhere but forget how to spell certain words.

■ Is your child aware that remembering things is important?

■ Does your child know he can develop "tricks" for remembering certain things (e.g., leaving his lunch box on top of his homework the night before to remind him to take both to school)?

■ Does your child know that remembering requires mental effort and doesn't just come automatically?

■ Have you practiced memorizing things with your child (e.g., poems, songs, shopping lists)?

You can help your child remember by talking about how you remember certain things. Do you use lists? Or tricks? Many of us remember the names of the Great Lakes, for example, by the acronym "HOMES" (Huron, Ontario, Michigan, Erie, Superior). Calling your child's attention to such strategies for remembering will aid memory development. Do not pressure children to memorize, however, but encourage this skill by making it manageable and fun. Start with something small and build as you go along.

Problem-Solving Skills

Which of these two parents do you think might have a better student?

Family I

Child: *"Mom, I'm stuck. I can't figure out how to make this project come out right."*

Mom: *"Oh, here, let me do it for you. That's really too hard for someone your age."*

Family II

Child: *"Mom, I'm stuck. I can't figure out how to make this project come out right."*

Mom: *"That sure looks like a tough problem, but I'll bet you can do it. Let's think together about how you might try another way to get unstuck."*

Since the ability and willingness to attack new kinds of problems is strongly related to success in school, we might guess that Family II will have a more successful student in the long run.

- **If your child has trouble solving a problem on the first try, can she shift and try another way?** For example, if she has trouble putting a puzzle together by starting with the middle pieces, can she shift strategies and start with the outside edges? Helpful parents often suggest different strategies ("What if you started with the corners?") to help children learn that they can try alternative methods to make things work.

- **Does your child have confidence that he is a good problem solver?** Do you accept completed projects (from a mud pie to a calculus equation) positively? Do you compliment him on how hard he worked to finish them?

- **Does your child realize that it's up to her to solve problems?** Or does she know you will jump in and do it for her if she quits?

- **Does your child know how good it feels to find a solution after "messing up" several times?** Parents need to communicate that "good mistakes" for learning are okay, and that competence doesn't come automatically.

Mindfulness

New research emphasizes the importance of thinking about our own thinking (also called "metacognition"). Mindfulness is the ability to understand your own thought processes and to realize how your efforts are related to outcomes. Children who are mindful are able to take greater responsibility for their own learning. They evaluate their mistakes and the effectiveness of their learning strategies. If they have trouble with a paragraph in reading, for example, they can slow down, reread the passage and ask themselves questions to aid understanding.

■ **Does your child have the time and the quiet space to get acquainted with his own mind?** Sometimes boredom can be a route to new ways of thinking and creativity.

■ **Does your child hear you talk about the way you are thinking about certain things?** ("I wonder which decision I should make. Let's see, if I do *x, y* might happen, but if I do *a, b* might happen. I need to consider the alternatives.")

■ **Does your child know he is responsible for the quality of his work?**

> ### Example
>
> Child: *"Mom, the teacher gave us a really unfair test today."*
>
> Parent: *"I'm sorry you're feeling bad about the test. Is there anything you could have done to prepare yourself better?"*

■ **Does your child know that he must be able to talk about the ideas in books he reads, rather than just sounding out the words without much thought?**

Together, learning habits are the cornerstones of good learning, and they arise directly from the various experiences and responsibilities that children have at home. School-smart parents (and teachers) consider these mental skills even more important than academic skills.

Social Skills

Social skills are another important component of school readiness—at any age. Children with good social skills can deal more confidently with their teachers, their peers and the school setting. Does your child:

■ get along with others?

■ understand that other people may have different points of view?

■ accept others who are different, whether in appearance, abilities or anything else?

■ show courtesy and respect to adults and other children?

■ know how to work as part of a group?

■ enjoy playing and socializing with other children?

■ stand up for herself in conflict, such as when she is teased?

■ know how to disagree tactfully?

■ know when to seek appropriate help from an adult when a situation gets out of hand (such as constant bullying)?

■ stand by her ideas and convictions when challenged?

■ feel okay about not always being included in a group?

■ feel okay about saying no when she doesn't want to be involved?

Children who can handle these situations appropriately have skills that will serve them well throughout life. The following are several methods to help your children of any age improve their social skills:

■ **Model good social skills in front of your children.** Pay attention to your own social behavior. What do your actions communicate to your child? Do you show respect and courtesy toward others, including children? How you deal with people and situations influences the development of your child's social skills. Talk to your child about why you do what you do. For example, when a friend is sick, let your child know that it is a sign of caring when you call to see how your friend is doing and to offer your help. Let him hear you make the call.

> ### Example
>
> *"Hello, Suzanne? Are you feeling any better today? Is there anything I can take care of for you while you're out sick?"*

■ **Encourage interaction with playmates and peer groups.** Children learn much about getting along with others from interacting with playmates and in groups. Make sure your child has ample opportunities to play with others after school and on weekends. Clubs and other after-school activities provide ready-made social situations. If your child is shy, offer a choice among several groups. Keep encouraging.

> ### Example
>
> *"I know you really enjoy making art projects at school, and Mrs. Barker told me your class's Brownie troop does a lot of crafts projects. Would you like to attend a meeting and see if you like it?"*

■ **Teach how to resolve conflicts nonviolently.** You can teach even very young children that "We don't hit in our family. We solve problems." This means finding discipline methods other than spanking (see Chapter 4 for better alternatives). When children do hit, remove them from the situation for a period of time.

> ### Example
>
> *"Charles, you know the rule about no hitting. Please go to your room, and we'll discuss it later."*

Even more important, though, is to teach your child better ways to resolve conflicts. Showing young children how to share and take turns is a good first step.

> ### Example
>
> *"Audrey, what if you and Matt take turns with the punch ball so that you both get to play with it?"*

Help older children learn to calm down and consider a problem from other perspectives than their own.

> ### Examples
>
> *"I can tell you are really angry with your brother. Take a deep breath and tell me what happened."*

"I can understand why you'd be mad at him for shoving you. I guess he must have been pretty angry to behave that way. Do you have any idea why?"

Help your child look at how fights start. Draw her attention to how behavior such as name-calling and daring can provoke arguments.

Example

"So, he was mad that you wouldn't let him ride your new bike, and when you taunted him about not having a new bike, he pushed you. Do you think teasing him was a good idea?"

Then teach her how to look for alternatives that will satisfy all parties involved.

Example

"I wonder if you could let him ride your bike for a little while, just to try it. Then he can ride his own bike with you."

■ **Talk with your child about cooperation, friendship and getting along.** Be alert for chances to discuss how to be a friend and get along with others. The stories that you read to your child or listen to together are full of situations in which characters either cooperate or clash. Use these stories as springboards into your own discussions. Avoid lecturing. Keep the discussion two-way, ask questions and keep your own comments brief.

Example

"What are some qualities Dorothy had that made her such a good friend to the Scarecrow, the Tin Woodman and the Cowardly Lion? Why did they like her so much?"

Your child's own experiences offer the best opportunities to teach. Be careful not to dictate when helping him find solutions to situations, or the natural need for independence may lead your child in the opposite direction of what you advocate. Instead, help him find a strategy that feels right to him.

Example

"I'm not sure what you should do, but let's talk about some options. How can you be a good friend and help Gina on her assignment without giving her your answers?"

Talk with your child about the differences that exist among people. Help her understand that people of different races, religions, nationalities, abilities, ages and appearances all have something special to offer.

Example

"I was happy to see you listening to Mrs. Cross's story about when she was a little girl in England. I've learned a lot about World War II from listening to her talk about her childhood."

■ **Role-play difficult situations.** Sticky social situations—turning down a best friend's invitation in order to do something with another friend, for example—call for skillful behavior. Talking with your child about such situations is a good start. But you can go further by role-playing the circumstances, with your child playing herself and you taking the role(s) of everyone else. Go through several scenarios to enable your child to practice getting her words right. Such practice increases children's confidence in their ability to handle situations effectively.

■ **Help your child learn to be assertive.** Getting along with others and solving problems nonviolently does not mean letting others take advantage of you. You can help your children learn to stand up for themselves and to assert their rights and opinions without becoming aggressive. Look for opportunities to discuss with your children the importance of:

● standing up for your own ideas and beliefs without putting down someone else's.

● asking for what you want without being a bully or dictator.

● saying "no" when you want to say "no" instead of just going along; saying "no" in a way that preserves a relationship if you want to keep it intact.

● saying "yes" when you want to say "yes" instead of being too shy to accept a reasonable offer.

● disagreeing with another's point of view tactfully.

● knowing when and how to seek help from an adult.

Help your children gain confidence in their own ideas by encouraging everyone in your family to think for themselves.

Examples

"That's an interesting theory. Tell me more about how it would work in our own town."

"You have an interesting idea. Can you think of any problems that might arise if the school made after-school activities a requirement for every student?"

Look for these and other opportunities to help your children build strong social skills. You may be surprised to find that these skills not only help your children get along better with others, but also add to their academic success.

Chapter 2

A home that supports children as students contributes significantly to their school success. Laying the groundwork for this home involves meeting children's physical needs and providing the right environment. Nowadays, with busy parents and children running in all directions, these "basics" sometimes get neglected. If they do, your child already has several strikes against her. For example, the effects of inadequate sleep or nutrition sometimes masquerade as a learning disorder. Households that lack structure and organization or positive encouragement tend to produce disorganized or unmotivated students. Meeting children's needs requires attention from busy parents, but it's worth the effort.

Healthy Bodies/Healthy Minds

First Things First:

- Does your child have regular physical exams, which include proper immunization?

- Does your child have regular dental exams?

- Have you taken your child for eyesight and hearing checkups?

- If your child has a medical problem, such as diabetes or allergies, that requires medication, do he and the teacher understand the proper treatment procedures needed at school?

Nutrition

The brain can be as little as two percent of body weight, yet it uses up as much as 20 percent of the body's energy. Proper nutrition gives your child the fuel to maximize that energy and to perform well physically and academically.

Many children and adults who routinely fill up on foods high in fat and sugar wonder why they have trouble concentrating or staying alert over time. Once they change to a healthy diet and regular exercise program, they report being amazed at how much better they feel. They no longer lose energy easily and find they can work at peak performance for much longer stretches. Use the following guidelines to help your children improve their well-being and performance.

■ **Avoid junk food.** Too much sugar (or even artificial sweetener) may be a problem for some children, making it harder for them to focus on school work. Since most kids get about 25 to 33 percent of their calories from snacking, make sure you offer healthy alternatives to chips, candy and other sugar and salt addictives. Fruit, nuts, peanut butter, raw vegetables and fruit juices are good choices. Avoid using junk food as a reward and be on the lookout for "hidden" junk food, such as canned fruits and flavored yogurt, which can have a high sugar content, or artificially sweetened soft drinks, which may also contain caffeine.

Encourage your children to consider their own eating choices and to practice some self-discipline when it comes to junk food. Talk to them about the connection between what goes into their bodies and how they feel and react.

Example

"Do you remember, Allison, how nervous you were before that big test? You didn't eat breakfast, and then you had a soda and candy bar at school. I wonder if the caffeine in your soda and candy on an empty stomach made you even more nervous than you already were."

■ **Study food package labels**. While it is probably not practical to eliminate all the junk food your kids eat (such as fast-food menu items), you can increase the healthy food they eat at home by making use of the excellent labeling information now required on all food packaging. Reading labels and choosing foods carefully can help you reduce the amounts of saturated fat, sodium and sugar in your family's diet. Reading labels also helps you provide the minimum daily requirements of vitamins and minerals in the foods you serve. These recommended levels can also be found in the labeling information.

■ **Balance menus from the basic food groups.** No longer do doctors advise basing eating choices on the traditional four food groups. Instead, they recommend the "Food Guide Pyramid" as a guide to more nutritious eating.

THE FOOD GUIDE PYRAMID

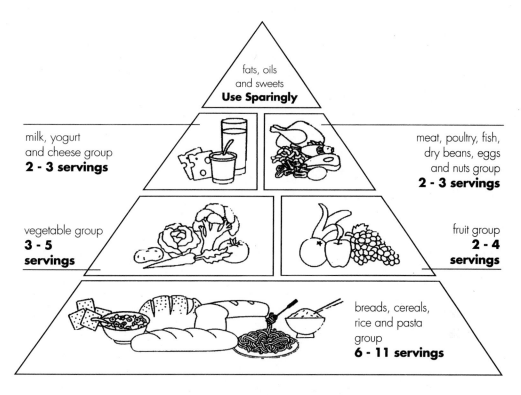

Source: U.S. Department of Agriculture, U.S. Department of Health and Human Services.

■ **Make breakfast, lunch and dinner the core of your family's healthy diet.** Experts disagree about the importance of breakfast. Some view it as overrated, a throwback to farm days when people worked for three hours in the field before coming in for a huge meal. Still, most experts agree that some fuel early in the day helps provide energy throughout the morning. Also, it is very important that children get some protein (peanut butter, cheese, milk) at breakfast. And eating even a light breakfast helps reduce the likelihood of overeating at lunch.

Research suggests that most kids get a more nutritious lunch from a school lunch program than from brown bagging it from home. If you do prepare your child's lunches, you can make them nutritious by providing sandwiches with lean meats, salads, fruit and vegetables.

Dinnertime is the one opportunity many families have to eat together. As such, it's a time for family sharing as well as physical sustenance. The exact time your family eats dinner is less important than the fact that it is regularly scheduled. If your family eats dinner late, make sure you offer healthy snacks to hold your children over. If you have toddlers, have them join you at the big table. It may be troublesome in the short run, but they will learn a lot from watching how the big kids and grownups conduct themselves. Warning: Taste food before serving it to toddlers to make sure it is not too hot.

Keep desserts as healthy as possible. Low-fat fruit yogurt, fruit or frozen fruit-cicles are good choices. Keep portions small, and make sure children have eaten the healthy foods first. Be careful not to bribe with dessert ("If you eat your dinner, you can have some of that delicious chocolate cake that Aunt Anita made."). Often bribery teaches children to focus on dessert even more, as dinner becomes something they must endure for the anticipated treat at the end.

■ **Don't force your children to eat.** This is a sure way to turn them off of the foods you are pushing—and even off of eating in general. (Remember when you were a kid and somebody tried to get you to eat liver and you gagged?) Instead, give children a choice between finishing their meals or waiting until the next one. As long as they aren't allowed to skip to dessert, their bodies will soon begin craving the nutritious food you have prepared.

Encourage your children to try new foods, but don't push them to clean their plates. If you have trouble getting your children to eat vegetables, try serving the vegetables as an appetizer before the meal, when children are hungriest. You may have more success with reluctant eaters if you consider their own tastes when planning meals. Older kids can actually help you plan menus, shop and cook.

■ **Make mealtimes as relaxed and pleasant as possible.** Family mealtimes can be occasions for stimulation of mental circuits as well as taste buds. Keep these times free from confrontation, major problem solving and labor negotiations. Turn off the phone and the TV, and be sure to include your children in conversation. Establish a special family dinnertime for conversation (at least once a week), and then stick to it. The priority you give it will show your children that talking and thinking together are important in your family (and two of the best ways for children to develop language and thinking skills; see Chapter 7).

Exercise

Another way to supply the brain with energy is through exercise. The deep breathing we do during exercise oxygenates the blood flowing to the brain. Oxygen helps brain cells work vigorously and efficiently, so exercise may prime the system for learning. Exercise seems to help activate brain chemicals for better attention and memory in class, and it dissipates the "wigglies" that strike so many children (particularly boys) when they have to sit for a long time. Children who are

physically fit are also more likely to participate in such school activities as games, dances and sports, all of which promote a positive social life.

Movement and physical activity as a part of learning are also important. For preschoolers, touching, feeling, manipulating and experimenting with the physical world are essential as the foundations for higher-level thinking. New research has made us aware that elementary, middle and even high school students also learn and remember better if the learning is "hands-on"; that is, if they work on a project, dramatize an idea or construct a model in addition to reading from a book or listening to a lecture.

Yet despite all of these benefits, only 32 percent of U.S. children ages 6–17 meet minimum standards for cardiovascular fitness, flexibility and body strength, according to a recent national study. Up to 25 percent (11 million) of children in this country are obese. This is twice the number of obese children from only a decade ago. It is no wonder that 30 to 35 percent of U.S. school-aged children are at risk for heart or circulatory disease and premature death as adults.

Sadly, the overcompetitive nature of team sports in our society has much to do with children's aversion to physical activity. According to Dr. Kenneth H. Cooper, a nationally recognized leader in fitness and health, many children of average ability drop out of team sports at about age nine because they don't think they can compete with better athletes. Many of these same children are late bloomers who would have done well in a sport if they had felt less pressured and had been encouraged to stick with it until they matured. They might then have found that they enjoyed the sport and would have stayed fit in the process.

How much exercise is enough? Dr. Cooper recommends that children get at least three 30-minute periods of physical activity each week. The following suggestions can help you promote exercise as a regular and enjoyable part of your family's life.

- **Put your children in charge of their own fitness.** For example, help your children choose physical activities they can do on their own on a regular basis, from bike riding and basketball to organized team sports at a local youth center.

  - **Be a role model by exercising yourself.**

  - **Make exercise a family value by participating in sports and physical fitness activities together.**

  - **Coach a sports team on which your child plays.**

  - **Find activities that your children enjoy doing.** Exercise that is fun becomes a positive lifelong habit.

  - **Help your children focus on improving their personal best rather than on winning and losing or comparing themselves with others.** If your child plays in a sports league, for example, stress her individual progress and the improvement of the team rather than whether they win the championship.

  - **Encourage enrollment in community sports programs.**

● **Help your children develop and use a wall chart or other system to monitor progress**.

● **Turn off the TV.** As trite as it sounded when our parents said it, urge your children to "go outside and play."

Sleep

The mother who tells her whiny, tantrum-throwing two-year-old that he needs a nap because he is "acting tired" instinctively understands the relationship between sleep and behavior. When children do not get enough sleep, they become tired and irritable and their performance suffers. (This can be especially detrimental during test-taking, when a tired mind functions less efficiently.)

How much sleep is enough? Most experts recommend between eight and 10 hours a night for children. You can learn to evaluate your own children's sleep requirements by tuning in to signs of sleep deprivation. Reconsider your bedtime policies if your child:

▪ has trouble concentrating on studies and other mental tasks for more than a short period.

▪ moves around and fidgets more than usual.

▪ becomes easily frustrated.

▪ is irritable.

▪ falls asleep on the couch, at the dinner table or at her desk at school.

■ has great difficulty waking up in the morning.

■ has dark circles under her eyes.

If your child is not getting enough sleep, use the bedtime techniques presented later in this chapter and the encouragement and discipline skills described in Chapter 4 to help establish a more successful bedtime routine. You and your child will feel better.

The Right Start

How your children begin their day depends a lot on you. Try to keep early-morning chaos at a minimum. Get clothes, homework and basic breakfast preparations organized the night before. Do not start arguments or bring up emotionally loaded topics at breakfast, if possible. Talk to your children before they leave. Tell them how much you care for them and how happy you will be to see them at the end of the day.

Structuring the School-Smart Home

Psychologists have been curious for years why some parents seem to be able to raise good students and future good citizens, while others do not. Their studies show clearly that one of the main factors is a well-organized environment where parents are firmly (but kindly) in charge and where there are reasonable rules and realistic, clearly expressed expectations. We might characterize these qualities as follows:

■ **"In this household, there are reasonable rules that keep us all safe."** (As children get older, they will increasingly have a part in negotiating the rules.)

■ **"We expect you to do your best, but we are willing to listen and are anxious to help out if you have a problem."**

■ **"Life here proceeds according to a schedule.** We may have to change it depending on family and individual activities, but we'll all work together in the planning. There will be regular times for meals, homework and bedtime."

■ **"Because we care about how you do in school, we limit TV and video game times."** Guidelines for TV and video games vary greatly, but most families with successful students place limits on these activities. Some pediatricians suggest 10 hours total per week, while others recommend one hour on weeknights and more, if desired, on weekends. Many "school-smart" families watch interesting programs and films together and discuss, critique and expand on what they have seen. It is also advisable to discourage or prohibit children from having TV and video games in their rooms so you can better monitor viewing time and content.

■ **"We enjoy spending time with you in activities such as games, hobbies, reading, talking, taking walks and doing chores."** In Chapters 7 and 8 we'll see how family discussions and activities build academic skills as well as family togetherness.

When we give children the freedom to make choices within the comforting limits of a structure, we provide the best of both worlds.

Although we want children to learn to make choices, the freedom to choose is also anxiety-producing. When we give children the freedom to make choices within the comforting limits of a structure, we provide the best of both worlds.

Providing Structure

Some parents worry that too much structure can harm a child's development. Others are concerned about being too lax and not providing enough. As in most of life, moderation is the key. Structuring a child's every waking minute while you frantically cart him from one activity to the next is overdoing it and is likely to be counterproductive. Such children often feel overloaded (so do their parents!), unmotivated and depressed.

Many parents find it easy to develop structure for themselves and their children. They are used to using schedules, "to do" lists and other time-management aids. They are comfortable knowing that dinner, bedtime, etc. are at certain hours. If you are this kind of parent, watch that you are not providing too much structure. You may need to allow for flexibility in your family's routines. It's okay to make occasional exceptions to the schedule for special events or guests, for instance.

If you are a parent who has difficulty with time management and schedules, however, providing consistent structure for your children is not going to be easy. Taking a time-management course or reading a book on the subject would be an excellent investment for you and your family. In the meantime, try using some of the following ideas:

- Set a regular dinnertime.
- Develop a bedtime routine.
- Set a weekday morning routine.
- Plan some weekend and holiday activities.
- Hold a weekly family meeting.
- Help your child organize her room.

Let's look at each one of these ideas in more detail.

■ **Set a regular dinnertime**. Most professionals in the parenting field bemoan the fact that too few families regularly eat dinner together anymore. Why are they so concerned? Because a set dinnertime with the whole family:

● is a chance to wind down every day (this is no time to grill the kids!).

● provides physical sustenance and pleasure.

● is a prime time for family sharing.

● creates time for family conversation, one of the most effective ways children build language and thinking skills.

Even if everyone in your family can't get together during the week, try to honor a scheduled dinnertime on weekends.

■ **Develop a bedtime routine.** Many parents find that bedtime equals hassle time. Even if one of the laws of the universe is that kids resist going to bed, a routine that includes positive activities can keep problems at a minimum. With young children, a routine might go like this:

7:30   Bath. Allow time in the tub for playing with tub toys, a little music ("Splish, Splash, I Was Taking a Bath" works great) and even some horsing around with Mom or Dad.

7:45   Put on pajamas.

7:50   Brush teeth.

7:55   Story or reading time.

8:15   Prayers and/or other ending traditions.

8:20   Goodnight hugs and "I love you's."

For older children, simply knowing that they need to get ready for bed by a certain time each night may be enough structure for them to independently take a bath, brush their teeth, put on their pj's and so on. Even with these children, a little one-on-one time with a parent at bedtime is a comforting closure to the day. It's also a good time for sharing; you may learn a lot about your child during this relaxed time of the day. Plus, because talking to a parent beats going to bed, it may be the only time when your child will talk to you without one foot out the door, on her way to a more exciting option.

Bonus Reading Time

Bedtime is a great time to encourage the most important of all academic skills, reading. Many of us developed our joy for reading with the bedtime stories and books our parents shared in that quiet time just before sleep. Telling stories to your children, reading them a book, letting them read to you—all are wonderful ways to reinforce the power and pleasure of the written word. Even older children sometimes enjoy when their parents read them a book that's a little beyond their own reading ability.

You can often encourage older children to read more if you allow them a few extra minutes to read on their own after you've said goodnight. This "bonus time" should be allowed only when children finish their other bedtime jobs on time. Because almost all kids enjoy staying up a little later, they will come to associate reading with a fun, positive part of their day.

■ **Set a weekday morning routine.** A typical one might go like this:

6:30 - 7:00   Parents rise and get dressed.

7:00   The children's alarm clock goes off. Note that we didn't say Mom or Dad tries to get everyone out of bed. Many parents are surprised to learn that by the time children are in first grade, they should be starting to get themselves up. This habit helps develop responsibility at an early age.

7:00 - 7:20   Children wash up, brush teeth and get dressed. For children under six, you might still have to help. (Select and lay out clothes the night before.) As they are able, let children pick what to wear from choices that are appropriate for the day. If you have more than one child, you may need to help them schedule bathroom sharing so that the routine goes smoothly.

Meanwhile, Dad and/or Mom is preparing breakfast.

7:20 - 7:40   Eat a nutritious breakfast.

7:40   Out the door, in the direction of school.

Note: School books, homework, projects, etc. are organized and placed strategically close to the door the
night before.

■ **Plan some weekend and holiday activities.** Occasional planned
activities help balance unstructured free time. While overplanning
is a mistake, a prearranged fun activity over a weekend or during a
holiday gives children something to look forward to and helps keep
them from drifting through this long (to a child) period of time.
Talk as a family about what the weekend holds in store. Planning a
family outing to the park, the zoo or the grandparents can be
enriching for everyone. Write them on the family calendar.

■ **Hold a weekly family meeting.** Use the time to plan family
outings, handle problems between family members and discuss
topics of importance to each person. Though challenging to stick
with, the family meeting is a great way to create harmony and
structure. (For more on family meetings, see the *Active Parenting
Today Parent's Guide*, by Michael H. Popkin, Ph.D., Active
Parenting Publishers, Inc., 1993.)

■ **Help your child organize her room**. This is important, so take a
deep breath and keep reading. Learning to structure her living
space is a big asset for a child. Discovering that "everything has a
place and is in that place" can help a child be more effective at
home, at school and, later, at work.

You can help your child learn this skill by breaking down the
process into steps. Teach him how to make his bed, organize his
closet and shelves and come up with systems for placing all those
"things" that kids accumulate. One inexpensive way to help your
child create an organizational system is to collect and use

cardboard boxes. Together with your child, paint or wallpaper the boxes, then stack and label them for different needs. "School books," "toys," "art supplies" and "personal books" might be a start. Here's a creative project with a lot of relationship-building potential.

Adjust the Level of Structure as Needed

Children of different ages and temperaments require different amounts of structure. Some children have learned how to structure their own time and can handle more freedom. Others need the help of an adult to provide some outside limits. To determine how much structure your own child needs, gradually loosen the reins and see how she responds. Is she bored, restless, in trouble? Or is she managing well on her own? Adjust your level of involvement until your child seems capable of performing tasks effectively.

Homework

One of the best ways to make study a positive experience for you and your child is to apply the principles of organization and structure to the job. Here are some tips to consider:

The floor in front of the TV is not a good place to study.

■ **Help your child develop a work area.** Children usually do better when they have a private study area, safe from interruption. It does not have to be large, but ideally it should not be shared. If you do not have a desk, set up a card table. Some children prefer to work at the kitchen table. If your child is one of these, make the

kitchen off-limits to other family members during study time. Although the bed might be suitable for reading, it's not a good spot for writing. The floor in front of the TV is not a good place to study. Equip your child's study area with a good light, a clock, pencils, paper and other supplies. Get a large month-at-a-glance wall calendar to record work assignments and school-related activities and hang it in the study area. Help younger children fill it out.

■ **Agree on a regular time for studying.** Forcing yourself to sit down and do something you do not enjoy is tough, even for adults (which is why we have so many photos still to put into albums). Children have an even harder time. To help overcome this natural procrastination, schedule a set time each day for homework.

If you have more than one child doing homework, try to have all of them working at the same time. This arrangement provides a positive atmosphere and fewer distractions. (Parents get a break too!) To gain agreement, involve all your children in choosing the study time. If they absolutely cannot agree, try rotating study times on a weekly or monthly basis. Of course, you do have the option of letting each child choose his own time and monitoring each separately.

Some children do better when working in shorter stretches punctuated with breaks. If your child is one of these, help her organize homework into shorter work periods—perhaps 20 minutes—with time in between to play or exercise. The renewed energy can be helpful. Likewise, after sitting in class all day, most children can use some physical activity right after school, before sitting back down to homework.

While there is no set rule about how much homework is enough, the national PTA has devised some general guidelines. According to these, students in grades 1–3 should spend about 20 minutes a night on homework; children grades 4–6, about 40 minutes; and children grades 7–12, up to two hours a night. Remember, though, that these are only guidelines; many schools' policies for college-bound students in higher grades, for instance, are up to four hours a night.

Base study time on a specific, reasonable length of time, not on the amount of home-work.

Base study time on a specific, reasonable length of time, not on the amount of homework. Even when your child has no homework, he can use his study time for school-related activities. This policy will reinforce the study habit and help prevent him from rushing through homework in order to finish earlier. On the other hand, if your child works steadily but fails consistently to finish homework within a reasonable time limit, alert his teacher to the problem.

Provide a quiet environment for study. You can show your child that you value homework and respect her need to complete it effectively by keeping the house quiet during this period. One child we know complained that the TV in the family room was so loud that she couldn't concentrate on her homework. Particularly for those children sensitive to background noise, a noisy environment is a real distraction. For all children, a quiet home during homework time sends a very supportive message. You could even go one step further by making this a study time for the entire family. Parents might read a book or the newspaper while children complete their school assignments. The message that "we are a family of learners" will be received loud and clear. Even a child who is too young for homework can use this quiet time for creative play.

For all children, a quiet home during homework time sends a very supportive message.

■ **Help your child develop a homework "to do" list.** Keeping track of homework assignments can be difficult for some students. Help your child develop a system for writing down assignments as the teacher gives them, then checking them off when completed. Such a "to do" list is not only an effective way to manage homework assignments, it also gives your children a productive system for tackling all kinds of work.

Home = A Place to Learn

Having worked to establish an environment that's "learning-friendly" for your child, how about making your home a place where adults are learning too? Stocking your house with plenty of books, newspapers and other reading material; limiting your own TV watching; and showing a curiosity and interest in the world around you tell children that learning is enjoyable and worth the effort it takes. Parents who like to learn usually have children who believe learning is important, who have a joy, curiosity and love of learning. Your attendance at a parenting course proves that you are still a motivated learner. You may even find the courage to sign up for some other form of adult education, either for credit or just for stimulation.

But learning isn't restricted to classrooms. You model learning for your child when you try a new dish in a restaurant, read for enjoyment or information, watch a documentary and comment on the ideas presented, plan a route on a map, study an insect in the grass, visit a museum or attend a performance. Explain to your child that new challenges can be hard at first, but that this is what makes them interesting or stimulating. Let your child see that you enjoy this process.

Ready for School—Ready to Learn

Going to school places many new demands on young children in particular. If we walk into any kindergarten or first grade, we can observe that some youngsters just seem more "ready" for school learning than others. If you have a young child, use this checklist to see if your home provides the ingredients for school "readiness":

1. Sufficient rest and nourishment to concentrate for several hours.
2. The experience of listening, following directions and responding politely to adults.
3. Knowledge of appropriate behavioral limits.
4. The experience of socializing with other children.
5. Help in obtaining and organizing school supplies.
6. Clothing chosen because it is easy for the child to manage, not because it has a designer label or is cute.
7. Help in learning to express needs, concerns or questions independently.
8. Practice in holding small objects and manipulating scissors, glue, crayons, paint brushes, rulers. Practice in following a left-to-right pattern.
9. Understanding that books are interesting gateways to stories and information.
10. Physical and emotional safety.

(Material in "Ready for School—Ready to Learn" from *Your Child's Growing Mind*, by Jane M. Healy, Ph.D., Doubleday, Inc., 1994.)

Test-Taking

Test-taking is a skill, one that can be learned just as well as the academic subjects that tests measure. The Recommended Reading list at the end of this book provides excellent resources to help you and your children develop this skill. A few of the best tips follow. Go over these with your children and work together to adapt these hints to your children's individual learning styles.

Studying for the Test

- **Studying should begin soon after the school year starts.** Keep notes organized for review and keep up with homework.

- **Listen for hints from the teacher about what will be on the test.** Ask him for hints about where to concentrate your efforts.

- **Determine the most important information in your study material and learn that first.**

- **Begin your intensive studying early in the afternoon or evening before the day of the test.** (The exact time will depend upon the student's age, her regular study routine and the level of the test.)

- **Develop a practice test either alone or with a study mate.** You may want to write a list of questions that may appear on your test before you begin intensive studying, so the list can guide you through your studying. Or you might ask a friend to give you a practice test near the end of your studying in order to catch any final items you may have overlooked.

- **Use positive self-talk.** Research shows that students who study *and* work on their self-confidence perform better than those who study only. For example, thoughts such as "I am well prepared and will do fine on this test" can help maintain a calm and clear mind.

■ **Gather all test-taking materials the night before.** Having to borrow a pencil right before the test can break your concentration and get you off to a bad start.

■ **Don't stay up too late and eat a good breakfast**. On the morning of the test, you will perform better with a rested mind and an energized body.

Taking the Test

Phase 1: Review the Test.

■ **First and foremost, read the instructions very carefully and follow the directions exactly.** Missing something here can cost you dramatically. For example, your instructions might ask you to answer one of the following two essay questions; if you missed those instructions, you would waste half your test-taking time writing an unnecessary essay.

■ **Quickly read through the entire test, noting which questions are most difficult, which count the most and which you don't understand.**

■ **Ask questions about anything you don't understand.** Shy children may need to practice how to ask for clarification.

■ **Budget your time, allowing more time for essay questions.** ("I'll spend 10 minutes on the true/false section, 20 minutes on the multiple choice and 30 minutes on the essay.")

■ **Take a deep breath.** It will help you relax and think more clearly.

Phase 2: Take the Test.

- **Answer the easiest questions first.** Not only is this good time management, but it will also build confidence.

- **Go back to the more difficult questions, but don't spend too much time on any one question until you have completed all of the others.**

- **Write clearly.**

- **Pay attention to clues and key words in each question.** For example, some choices in multiple choice questions may be eliminated because they would make the completed sentence grammatically incorrect.

- **Put something down for every question even if you don't know the answer.** You may know more than you think you know. Note: Children may be instructed while taking standardized tests that incorrect answers will cost them more deductions than answers that they have left blank. Make sure you know the exact instructions for each test.

Phase 3: Review.

- **Review every item carefully before turning in your test.** You may catch a careless error or have a last-minute insight.

- **Use all of the time allowed.** The longer you review your answers, the more chances you have to discover mistakes.

Chapter 3

School-smart families know that when educators and parents work together cooperatively, the positive impact on children can be enormous. Developing a working relationship with your children's teachers helps you and the teachers better assess your children's readiness and ability to do the job. Parents then have a better idea where their help is needed, and children are more likely to feel comfortable at school when they sense the harmony between parent and

teacher. By following a few simple steps, you can establish open lines of communication with your children's teachers. Understanding their perspectives will help make your relationship productive and enjoyable.

Start the Year Out Right

Don't wait for a problem to come up before you connect. Most schools have "Back to School" nights or "Open House" early in the school year; make this an absolute must on your calendar! Many parents feel uneasy about going "back to school." They may put off contacting their child's teacher and become even more anxious if the teacher calls to request a meeting. These feelings are understandable if the parent's own school memories are negative ones (of a teacher who was overly stern or unfairly critical, for example).

It helps to remember that nowadays most teachers are parents, too. By and large, they care deeply about children, and they have their own apprehensions and uncertainties about how they will be viewed by you, the child's parents.

Parents will benefit from much that they hear in a back-to-school night setting. The better you know what your child will be learning and what the teacher expects, the better you will be able to support these plans. However, teachers differ greatly in the amount of information they wish to communicate about their plans for the year. Many teachers have the entire year's plan in mind in September, but others prefer to wait and judge what is most important for the needs of each class.

Listen attentively to what the teacher tells you; she will share what information she considers important. If you have a question, ask it in a friendly and polite manner. Obviously, you will not demand the teacher's time and attention in the middle of a group meeting to talk about your individual child. If important information remains uncovered after the meeting, try to schedule an appointment, at the teacher's convenience, for follow-up conversation. Always remember that your goal and the teacher's are mutual—to help your children succeed in school.

Questions to Ask Your Child's Teacher

The following are questions the teacher may answer:

■ **What's in the curriculum this year?** You are naturally interested in learning what subjects your child will be studying. Will he have different teachers for some of them? If so, write down their names. Will the curriculum cover any special topics or themes? Some teachers provide a list of books the students will read. You might want to read some of these yourself in order to talk about them with your child. Does the teacher plan to introduce any special long-term projects? Do you have any particular skills or knowledge, or is there anything you can do that might be helpful (such as bring in materials, contact outside speakers, arrange for food for a particular theme unit)?

■ **What supplies will your child need?** Your child's teacher may hand out a list of supplies that students must purchase (in many schools, this is available before the first day of school). You will also need to know of any special requirements for packing lunches or providing lunch or milk money. It's also helpful to learn about equipment needs for any projects that may come up during the year. (Otherwise, you may find yourself sitting in your bathrobe at 9:30 one night, only to have your child approach you and say that by tomorrow he must bring to science class a box that once held a refrigerator.)

■ **What is the teacher's homework policy?** Find out whether the teacher routinely assigns homework. How much time are students expected to spend on homework each night? Are homework assignment sheets passed out, or should the student keep notes on assignments each day? What does the teacher see as the parents' role in helping with homework? If special projects are planned, will your child require trips to the library?

■ **What is the teacher's policy regarding parents as school volunteers?** Most teachers appreciate all the help they can get, and parents may be encouraged to volunteer time as helpers. For example, parents might conduct book discussion groups (common in "whole language" classrooms), help in

the library, call other parents with information, drive on field trips or provide refreshments for special occasions. Many schools select "room parents" to be special helpers. If you can possibly manage the time, volunteer to help out. You don't need an advanced education or special skills to contribute, just the desire to help. In addition to having fun, you will make your child feel very proud of you.

How will parents be informed about additional school or classroom policies such as attendance, discipline, health and safety? Because school policy evolves as the needs of the situation demand, you will want to know how you can expect to stay informed. Does the school provide a back-to-school information kit that you can get (and read)? Will they send memos with your child or through the mail? Are school and classroom meetings the most likely source of this information?

How will the teacher judge your child's progress? When can you expect report cards, and what kind of grading system will be used? For example, the traditional A, B, C, D grading scale has recently been replaced in many schools by a more general system, such as Outstanding, Average and Needs Attention, or even by a system of thorough comments without categorical grades. Will assessments be based only on academic achievement, or will effort and attitude play a part?

What is the best way to exchange information? Tell the teacher how to reach you. Find out how best to reach him, in case it ever becomes necessary. Keep in mind that the teacher is very busy, as you are; in addition to working with your child, he confers with many parents. Ask the following questions to determine the most efficient way to maintain contact.

- Is it OK to call?

- If so, when?

- Is it best to put my concerns in writing?

- If so, do I send them to school with my child or mail them to you at school?

- To what address?

- What procedure should I follow if I need to set up a face-to-face conference?

- If I have a concern about issues outside the classroom, such as trouble on the school bus, should I contact you, the counselor or someone in the principal's office?

What to Expect at the Year's First Parent/Teacher Conference

Regularly scheduled parent/teacher conferences are a time-honored way to learn about a child's academic, social and emotional progress in school. Here are pointers to help make the parent/teacher conference a successful experience for everyone:

1. **Come prepared to listen.** Although these conferences can differ dramatically from one school (or even one classroom) to the next, one thing is invariable: You are going to hear about your children. Take seriously what the teacher tells you. Whether the report is glowing or indicates areas of concern, you will gain important information.

2. **Come prepared to share with the teacher any relevant information about your child, such as hobbies, interests or feelings toward school.**

3. **Share with the teacher how you feel the year is going.** Does your child enjoy all subjects (classmates, activities) this year? What's her attitude toward homework?

4. **Don't be afraid to ask questions:** "Why do you think Jennifer's having so much trouble with math?" "Would you like us to help George proofread his papers for spelling before he hands them in?"

5. **Compliment the teacher on something she's doing:** "I like the way you're encouraging the kids to write this year. It must take a lot of time to make all those comments." "Ellen appreciates the way you encourage students to speak up in class."

6. **Think carefully about how you will present the conference results to your child.** (Some schools now include children in the conference itself.) When you talk to your child afterwards, always start with something positive. Then explain tactfully any needs the teacher has emphasized. Let your child express his feelings, too, and reassure him that you will try to help when possible.

Inform the School of Your Child's Special Needs

Parents need to alert the school before the start of the year to any special needs of their children. Find out the school's procedure (be it a note or a phone call) for informing the teacher if your child:

■ has poor vision or hearing.

■ has other physical problems, such as allergies.

■ needs special medication (including instructions for administrating or possible side-effects).

■ has particularly strong fears about such things as intimidation by other students.

■ has a diagnosed learning disability.

■ is experiencing stress or grief over such events as family problems, a recent move or the death of a pet.

Maintain a Good Relationship All Year

Once you have gotten the school year off to a positive start by developing a working relationship with the teacher(s), it's up to you to continue to make yourself available, offering help and support as the year progresses.

■ **Keep the teacher informed of when and where you are available to help out, depending on your work or home schedule.**

■ **Respond promptly to notes or calls from the school (don't force the teacher to send follow-up notes).**

■ **Let your child know that you and the teacher are in contact and that you support the teacher.** A first simple step is to highlight good news from school. Look for opportunities to make comments such as, "Your teacher says you are really making an effort. That makes me proud." Your attitude about the teacher is all-important. Whether or not children like and respect their teachers often depends on their parents' views of those teachers.

Cooperative Problem Solving

Wise parents let teachers know that they would like to be notified by the middle of a grading period if a child is experiencing academic difficulty. They also make it clear to both teacher and child that they want to be informed promptly of any social or behavioral problems. Make sure the teacher knows you are genuinely concerned about your child's progress and willing to do all you can to help. In Chapters 7 and 8 we will look at steps to take if your child runs into specific academic difficulties.

If You Suspect Teacher/Child Troubles

Unfortunately, trouble at school can sometimes also mean problems with your child's teacher. On the rare occasions when a parent has good reason to believe that a teacher is not doing the job properly or is treating a child unfairly, take action but proceed with caution. First, watch for these red flags:

1. **Repeated negative incidents related to the teacher's methods or behavior, reported by your child and verified by responsible children or adults.**

2. **Abusive comments written by the teacher on work papers brought home by your child.**

3. **Sudden and unexplained changes in attitudes or behavior, or physical symptoms (e.g., frequent stomachaches) in your child.** (Note: Such changes are more often related to other causes, such as undiagnosed learning or emotional problems, so *do not assume such changes alone signal a problem with the teacher.*)

If a problem has persisted for several weeks, schedule a conference with the teacher. You may want to ask at the conference for a chance to observe your child in the classroom. (This will depend upon your schedule and the school's policies.) Sometimes this much attention eliminates the problem, and parents may learn to their surprise that their child's behavior is actually the source of the trouble. These are sensitive issues, and you do not want to alienate the teacher, so use your good judgment in deciding on a course of action.

If the situation does not improve, schedule an appointment with the principal, school counselor or school psychologist. State your case clearly, using as much objective evidence as you have been able to accumulate. If the difficulty results from a personality conflict between your child and a particular teacher, your principal should be able to suggest helpful solutions. A change of classroom may be the last resort. If the problem is more extensive and more than one family is involved, make a group appointment to see the principal.

Your degree of involvement will vary according to your child's age. If your child is of preschool or early elementary age, be very attentive. Young children are not good factual reporters and often blame themselves rather than perceive the unrealistic or overly punitive nature of an adult's demands.

If your child is of older elementary school age, you still have the major responsibility to see that he is in a positive and healthy educational environment. However, as with teenagers, we want to encourage elementary-age children to take increasing responsibility in "fighting their own battles." Learning to get along with difficult people (such as teachers or bosses) is an important lesson, but we still must keep an eye out for situations in which the youngster is truly unable to cope. Incompetent teachers are rare, so if you are like most parents, you will never need to intervene in such a situation.

Cooperative Problem-Solving Model

No matter what the difficulty, it is helpful to have a system to follow if trouble arises. Here is a useful one if you need to meet with any school professionals about your child.

1. Set up a meeting with the teacher.
2. Focus on your common goal to help your child succeed.
3. Write down your concerns before you get to the meeting.
4. Ask the teacher how she sees the problem.
5. Find the common ground.
6. Bring a solution, not just a problem.
7. Agree on a course of action.
8. Agree on how you will follow up.
9. Monitor progress.
10. Evaluate the situation at a follow-up meeting.

Let's take a closer look at each of the steps.

1. **Set up a meeting with the teacher.** The best way to handle a concern is to be direct. Most teachers appreciate parents who come directly to them so that together they can find a solution. In many cases, problems are not as great as you first imagine. Simple, open communication is often enough to correct them. Be sure to call ahead to schedule a conference, because "drop-in" meetings are often rushed and put an unfair time burden on the teacher.

> **Example**
>
> *"Hello, Mrs. Hickman? This is Michael's mother, Janice Edwards. I'd like to schedule an appointment with you to talk about some concerns I have about Michael."*

2. **Focus on your common goal to help your child succeed.** Cooperation will produce better solutions than an adversarial approach, and it will help you maintain a positive relationship with your child's teacher. By making the *problem* your enemy—not each other—you will do much toward helping your child.

> **Example**
>
> *"I know that we both want Michael to have a good year, so I thought we should talk about some things together."*

3. **Write down your concerns before you get to the meeting.** Taking the time to do this provides some perspective, helps calm emotions, allows you to clarify the issues and gives you an opportunity to think about possible solutions. Having these notes with you during the conference will enable you to cover the concerns that are important to you without becoming sidetracked.

> ### Example
>
> *Concerns about Michael*
>   1. *He said that some of the boys are picking on him on the way to class.*
>   2. *He said that Mrs. Hickman didn't care or do anything about it when he told her.*
>   3. *He said that she didn't like him.*

4. **Ask the teacher how she sees the problem.** After you have calmly shared your concerns with the teacher, it is important for you to ask how she sees the problem. Her perspective is critical for problem solving. Also, inviting the teacher's views says that you realize there is more to the situation than you alone could know. Really listen to the teacher as she gives her point of view. Avoid getting defensive or aggressive. Remember, the purpose of the meeting is to help your child, who may have problems that you don't know about.

> ### Example
>
> *"I know that children see things from their own perspective, so I was hoping you could tell me more about the situation as you see it."*

5. **Find the common ground.** The most effective approach to problem solving is to focus the discussion on what the two of you agree on, rather than on what you see differently. Then together you can look for common solutions to your concerns.

Example

"I can see that we agree on a couple of things. One, that Michael can be pretty aggressive himself and needs to work on getting along with these boys better. And two, that when you encouraged him to work out a solution for himself, it didn't mean that you didn't care or like him."

6. **Bring a solution, not just a problem**. Although you won't have all the facts before the conference, you can still brainstorm possible solutions to the problem before your meeting. Your suggestions let the teacher know that you are not just criticizing, but that you want to work with him to improve the situation. You may find yourself modifying your original solution as you listen to the teacher's point of view.

Example

I'm not sure of the best solution to this problem, but I have an idea that I'd like your opinion about. Would it be possible for you to spend a little time talking with Michael about how he could handle the situation better? This would let him know that you really do care. And I think your coaching would be a big help to him."

7. **Agree on a course of action.** Once you have discussed some possible solutions to the problem, agree on a plan of action. What will you do to help solve the problem? And what will the teacher do? A coordinated effort between home and school usually has a greater impact than one person working alone—it's certainly better than two people working against each other.

> ### *Example*
>
> *"So we agree that you'll do a little coaching of Michael at school, and we'll do the same at home. I also like your suggestion that Michael and I read that story together about the boy who always had to have his own way. That should make for a good family talk."*

8. **Agree on how you will follow up.** The best-laid plans of parents and teachers often go astray when nobody bothers to follow up. Contact each other after you've had a chance to put your plan into action. This allows you and the teacher to evaluate how the plan is working and to make corrections if necessary. It also helps motivate both parties to follow through with their agreement.

> ### *Example*
>
> *"Great. I'll call you in two weeks, about 8:30 at night on the 22nd, to see how it's going. And of course, call me whenever anything comes up that you think I should know about."*

9. **Monitor progress.** Looking for signs that the situation is improving can help you see where to fine-tune the plan and is a great motivator to continue in the right direction. Create a simple chart on which you can record your child's progress. If your child is involved in the plan, create the chart together and let him mark his progress with you. Buy some stickers, or use simple check marks.

If your child is involved in the plan, create the chart together and let him mark his progress with you.

> ### *Example*
>
> *"Okay, we will both keep track of how many times Michael complains about being picked on. Then we'll compare notes*

when I call. I'll also talk with him about setting up a chart at home called "Getting Along." Every day he tells me that he got along well at school—that is, no one picked on him—we'll put a star on the chart."

10. Evaluate the situation at a follow-up meeting. Some problems are harder to solve than others, and not all first tries are successful. Therefore, it's important to evaluate realistically how the situation has evolved since you put the plan into action. If the plan is going well, enjoy your joint success, express your appreciation and move on. If the problem persists, repeat the cooperative problem-solving process, looking for other alternatives. Some situations may require input from other professionals. School counselors, psychologists and social workers are a few of the resources you may have available to help. Talk with the teacher about this possibility.

Example

"I heard from Michael that your coaching talks went really well, and I'm glad to hear from you that he complained only one time the first week and none since then. The charting at home seemed to help too. At least he was enthusiastic about putting his stars on. Thank you so much for your help on this. We're all really fortunate to have you as Michael's teacher."

Know and Support the School's Discipline Plan

All schools need the support of parents in order to maintain a reasonably disciplined environment for students and faculty. Get to know your school's discipline plan. If it is in writing, ask for a copy from the office. Take it home and go over it with your children. It may not be exactly as you might write it, but unless it contains techniques or approaches that you strongly oppose, you want to help your child learn to live within its guidelines. If your school does not have a written plan, ask your child's teacher to explain what discipline methods she uses in her classroom and the school's approach to discipline.

If you are strongly opposed to parts of the plan, you may want to call the principal for a meeting to discuss your concerns. If you tend to become easily angered and indignant, be sure to calm yourself before calling for such a meeting. A positive relationship between you and the school is important for your child and your family. Taking a hostile approach is likely to make the administration defensive and undermine your effectiveness. Besides, such an approach is unfair. You haven't heard the school's side yet. Listen with an open mind to the school's point of view; you may agree with their policies more than you think. Stay calm and look for solutions. For best results, we recommend using the cooperative problem-solving approach described in this chapter to find a common ground.

Be especially on guard against degrading the school's discipline policy in front of your child. This may send the message that your child doesn't have to follow the rules or accept the teacher's authority. If she already has trouble with authority, she may interpret your anger as license to further rebel. Such escalation of the problem is not in your or your child's best interests. Be absolutely clear with your child that the school has the legitimate authority to set policy, and that unless that policy can be changed, it is up to her to abide by the rules in effect.

Understanding Information from the School

One of the best ways to learn about your child's abilities is to pay close attention to any information from the school. You also have a legal right to see any information about your child that the school keeps on file. Many school districts keep a "cumulative file" that travels with your child from year to year. In it are kept records of report cards and possibly some "standardized tests" given to large groups of students. These tests compare your child's progress to the average for an age or grade. The tests may be either of "aptitude"  (e.g., tests of IQ, special abilities, career aptitudes) or "achievement" (e.g., the level of reading, math, science the child has mastered).

Districts and states vary widely in their choice of tests and the manner in which results are used or reported to parents. Many schools have discontinued the use of IQ tests, for reasons you will soon understand. If you have concerns about testing, you may ask your principal about the school's policy, but most parents feel they are adequately informed by regular reports from the teacher. Sometimes, however, school information is difficult to decipher. Here's a brief primer.

Aptitude Tests

Aptitude tests are those which attempt to measure a child's basic intelligence (IQ), interests or learning skills, such as language or perceptual abilities. While some types of IQ tests can be very useful to a trained psychologist, these tests have come under fire recently because they are not always fair to children of varying cultures, their results don't seem to be terribly good predictors of life-long success and they have too often been used inappropriately to assign labels (e.g., "mentally retarded") to children.

As psychologist Howard Gardner has pointed out, "intelligence" is much more complicated than anything that can be tested in a brief time, and experts are still arguing about just what it is! Since students with a high level of motivation and good habits for learning make liars out of these tests every day, we know we still have a lot to learn about "aptitude."

Here are some aptitude test guidelines to consider:

- **Don't ever allow an important decision about your child to be made on the basis of one test or one person's opinion.**

- **Group IQ tests, which are given to a whole class at a time and use machine-scored, pencil-and-paper answer sheets, are notoriously unreliable measures of intelligence.**

- **If a child needs special testing to assess learning abilities, disabilities or placement in a special program, you should request a complete *psychoeducational evaluation* by a trained professional.** This evaluation should be conducted within a reasonable time frame by the school personnel at no cost to you. If for any reason this type of testing is not available, you have the right to seek an outside evaluation from a qualified professional or clinic.

This evaluation should include (but not be restricted to) an *individual* IQ test, in which child and examiner meet privately to do several different types of learning/thinking activities. It should also include thorough assessments of the child's academic progress and tests of various processing abilities (how well your child understands and uses language, remembers different types of material or coordinates visual and motor learning, for example). This more extensive testing can show a useful profile of your child's learning abilities.

- **If your child has been tested and you do not understand what the results mean, don't hesitate to ask questions until the information is properly explained.** You have the legal right to request a conference to share the results of any testing or evaluation given to your child.

- **If qualified professionals make recommendations for your child on the basis of a thorough evaluation, pay attention and try to follow up on their suggestions.** They should also help you understand the school's goals and keep you informed about your child's progress.

Achievement Tests

These measures try to find out how much the student has learned in specific subjects. You may remember sitting down with an entire roomful of your classmates and taking achievement tests in which you marked the proper answer by filling in a "bubble." Educators' dependence on such achievement tests is declining, as we realize what a narrow view it gives us of how much a child has really learned.

Commonly Used Tests

Most schools now use more than one means of assessing what children have learned:

- **Standardized tests:** usually "fill in the bubble" or essay questions given to groups of students.

- **Individual assessments:** the teacher meets with each child to determine what she has learned in specific subjects.

- **Teacher-made tests:** these more closely reflect the important skills and knowledge taught in the course.

- **Performance-based assessments:** the child keeps a portfolio of work throughout the year and is usually asked to prepare some sort of project or write an essay that reflects her understanding of the material.

Most educators now believe it is important to get as many views of a child as possible. Parents should support a wide and fair assessment program in schools. Parents should also:

1. pay close attention to reports about testing that come home from school.

2. attend any parent-teacher conferences that are scheduled.

3. ask questions. "What do these scores mean?" is good for starters.

If you still have serious questions about the way your child is being viewed or evaluated at school, request a conference with the teacher, school counselor, principal or psychologist and state your concerns. Remember, again, that you have a right to see the contents of any files of information that the school keeps on your child.

If You Suspect a Learning Difference

Start to ask questions about a possible *learning disability* if your child has persistent and unusual difficulty mastering certain subjects, such as reading or math, or skills, such as handwriting or spelling. Learning disabilities (or "learning differences," as some of us prefer to call them) show up in otherwise able children. They are usually diagnosed on the basis of a significant difference between the child's overall intelligence and her performance in specific subjects or skills. This does not mean you should hit the panic button if your child has a temporary difficulty with something in school. If the difficulty is persistent, however (over six months, at least), and especially if it shows up in several areas, you may need to initiate some action.

Do not hit the panic button if your child has a temporary difficulty with something in school.

Many children go through temporary difficulties due to emotional concerns, social problems or preoccupying family issues. These problems should not be confused with a learning disability. Other children are simply immature—they may be potentially excellent students, but their brains are not ready for grade-level work. These students often end up looking "learning disabled" if someone tries to push them too hard or too soon. An immature child who is displaying some of the danger signs listed on the next page, however, should also receive a thorough evaluation.

Danger Signs

How do you know if your child needs to be evaluated for a learning difference? Look for several of these danger signs that persist:

- A negative attitude toward school.

- Physical symptoms not explained by physical causes (e.g., stomachaches, sleep problems, general "I don't feel good" complaints before going to school in the morning).

- Family history of learning problems, late reading, poor spelling, unusual difficulty with math.

- Significant development lags in language, motor coordination, social skills or other areas.

- Unexplained difficulty with specific school subjects, particularly oral reading, writing, spelling or math in an otherwise able child.

- Persistently "lost" homework or homework that is clearly too difficult for the child.

- "Laziness," "sloppiness," "careless errors"—terms often applied to a struggling youngster who actually needs specialized teaching and help.

- Serious difficulty listening, paying attention, remembering or organizing possessions and thoughts.

- A combination of unusual difficulty in relating to other people, making friends and understanding concepts presented.

■ Continual behavioral changes, mood swings and interpersonal difficulties.

How to Seek Help

Chapters 7 and 8 outline procedures for specific academic subjects. Here are some general guidelines:

1. **Make an appointment with the teacher** to describe your concerns.

2. **Request specialized testing** from the school reading specialist, psychologist or speech/language therapist.

3. **Consider an outside evaluation** from a clinic or private educational therapist. Your best bet is the type of psychoeducational evaluation previously described in Aptitude Tests. The accompanying report should contain recommendations to help the school and the teacher deal more effectively with the child.

Teachers and administrators are in the business to help children, but they can get overwhelmed by the magnitude of their jobs. Your role as advocate and cheering section for your child can make the difference between a positive and a negative outcome. No matter what else happens, your primary assignment is to:

■ **Continue to reassure your child that she is okay, and that you love her no matter what.**

■ **Try to avoid adversarial relationships**. You, the school and your child all need to work together for positive results.

■ **Make your home environment "school-smart" by following the guidelines in this book.** Children with learning differences need extra-special conversational attention, clear limits on TV and structured homework situations.

If you have a child with a learning difference, please believe that many such individuals have achieved notable success in the arena of life.

If you have a child with a learning difference, please believe that many such individuals have achieved notable success in the arena of life. Use the Recommended Reading list for follow-up reading, and enjoy the many special talents of this special person in your household.

SEVEN FORMS OF INTELLIGENCE

Think about each of your own strengths and how well you learn in each of the seven styles. Fill in the chart under the column marked "parent." Then consider each of your children, filling in the chart according to how you view their strengths. Compare where you are alike and where you are different. Use this information to build your children's strengths and to encourage growth in areas where they are less interested. Be on guard to avoid undervaluing areas in which they are strong and you are less interested.

Rate each type of intelligence (S=Strong; M=Moderate; U=Uninterested)

Learning Style	Parent	Child 1	Child 2	Child 3
1. Linguistic	_____	_____	_____	_____
2. Logical or Mathematical	_____	_____	_____	_____
3. Musical	_____	_____	_____	_____
4. Spatial or Visual	_____	_____	_____	_____
5. Kinesthetic	_____	_____	_____	_____
6. Interpersonal	_____	_____	_____	_____
7. Intrapersonal	_____	_____	_____	_____

ASSESSING YOUR CHILDREN'S LEARNING HABITS

Consider each of the learning habits discussed in Chapter 1 as they relate to your children. Evaluate your children's strengths in each area by marking an "E" for excellent; "S" for satisfactory or "N" for needs work. Then look for opportunities to build on strengths and work on weaknesses.

	Child 1	Child 2	Child 3
MOTIVATION			
Child believes that her efforts make a difference and that she can succeed if she tries.	_____	_____	_____
Child believes it's worth trying even if it's hard, because it makes her feel successful.	_____	_____	_____
Child believes being smart is not just something she is born with, but something she can develop through her own efforts.	_____	_____	_____
ATTENTION			
Child can stick with a project or task for a reasonable length of time.	_____	_____	_____
Child can persist if a task doesn't come easily.	_____	_____	_____
Child can shift attention when needed.	_____	_____	_____
LANGUAGE			
Child can listen and remember what he hears.	_____	_____	_____
Child can express an idea with reasonable ease.	_____	_____	_____
Child can ask questions to get information.	_____	_____	_____

	Child 1	Child 2	Child 3
Child can take turns appropriately in conversations.	_____	_____	_____

MEMORY

Child is aware that remembering things is important.	_____	_____	_____
Child uses memory "tricks" to remember certain things.	_____	_____	_____
Child knows that remembering takes effort.	_____	_____	_____

PROBLEM SOLVING

Child will try alternative ways to solve a problem.	_____	_____	_____
Child has confidence that she is a good problem solver.	_____	_____	_____
Child realizes that it's up to her to solve her own problems.	_____	_____	_____
Child knows that it feels good to solve a problem after "messing up" several times.	_____	_____	_____

MINDFULNESS

Child takes the time to think about things.	_____	_____	_____
Child hears parents talk about the way they think about things.	_____	_____	_____
Child knows that he is responsible for the quality of his work.	_____	_____	_____
Child knows he must be able to talk about the ideas in what he is reading (rather than sounding out words without much thought).	_____	_____	_____

PHYSICAL NEEDS CHECKLISTS

In order to receive the full benefit from your effort to help them succeed, your children need proper nutrition, exercise and sleep. The following checklists will help you determine whether your children are receiving these physical basics.

The Basics

If you answer "no" to any of the following questions, call your doctor for more information on these crucial aspects of your children's health.

YES or NO

1. Do your children have regular physical exams, which include proper immunization?   _____

2. Do your children have regular dental exams? (Check with your dentist to find out if she recommends checkups every six months or once a year.)   _____

3. Have you taken your children for eyesight and hearing checkups?   _____

4. If your children have medical problems, such as diabetes or allergies, that require medication, do both they and their teachers understand the proper treatment procedures needed at school?   _____

Nutrition
Answer "yes" or "no" to the following statements. A "no" answer on any item indicates an area that needs work.

YES or NO

1. For snacks, I make available healthy alternatives to junk food such as fruit, vegetables and peanut butter. _____

2. I read and consider food package labels when I buy groceries in order to reduce the amount of saturated fat, sodium and sugar my family eats. _____

3. Breakfast, lunch and dinner are the core of my family's diet. _____

4. Our family eats balanced meals that include the recommended number of servings of grains, fruit and vegetables, protein (such as meat) and dairy products. _____

5. Our family eats dinner together at least once a week. _____

6. Mealtimes at my house are relaxed and pleasant. _____

Exercise
Answer "yes" or "no" to the following statements. A "no" answer on any item indicates an area that needs work.

YES or NO

1. Our family exercises for 30 minutes, at least three times a week. _____

2. Our family participates in sports and physical fitness activities together. _____

3. My children enjoy exercising. They believe staying
   fit is fun!   _____

4. Our family uses a wall chart to monitor fitness
   progress and to motivate us to keep exercising.   _____

5. I encourage my children to focus on improving
   their personal best rather than on winning and
   losing or comparing themselves with others.   _____

Sleep

Answer "yes" or "no" to the following questions. If you answer "yes" to any item on the list, your child may not be getting enough sleep.

Does your child:

	Child 1	Child 2	Child 3
1. have trouble concentrating on studies and other mental tasks for more than a short period?	_____	_____	_____
2. move around and fidget more than other children her age?	_____	_____	_____
3. become easily frustrated?	_____	_____	_____
4. act irritable?	_____	_____	_____
5. fall asleep on the couch, at the dinner table or at his desk at school?	_____	_____	_____
6. have great difficulty waking up in the morning?	_____	_____	_____
7. have dark circles under her eyes?	_____	_____	_____

STRUCTURE SNAPSHOT

Because it is possible to provide too much or too little structure for your children, it is helpful to reevaluate from time to time the amount of structure that you provide. Try taking a "snapshot" of a typical day's structure for each of your children by filling out this schedule and answering the following questions. Then modify the structure as you think best.

Morning Routine

	Actual time	Are my children rushed?	Ways to improve
rise and shine	_____	_____	_____
wash up	_____	_____	_____
get dressed	_____	_____	_____
eat breakfast	_____	_____	_____
leave for school	_____	_____	_____

After-School Activities

	What do my children do?	Is this too much or too little structure?	Ways to improve
Monday	_____	_____	_____
Tuesday	_____	_____	_____
Wednesday	_____	_____	_____
Thursday	_____	_____	_____
Friday	_____	_____	_____

Dinnertime

Do we have a regular dinnertime? _____

What steps can we take to have a regular dinnertime? _____

How often do we eat together? _____

What could we do so that we eat together more often? _____

_____

Homework

Do my children have a set homework time? _____

Do my children have their own place for study? _____

Is the house quiet during this time? _____

Am I available to help if needed? _____

How can I modify homework time to make it more effective? _____

_____

Bedtime Routine

Do we have a regular bedtime routine? _____

If your answer is no, create your own routine, using the following suggestions as a guide.
Try it for one week, then evaluate and improve as needed.

Routine	Time	After 1 week, evaluate and suggest ways to improve
Bath and brush teeth	_____	_____
Talking or other calming activity	_____	_____
Story or reading	_____	_____
Prayers or other good-night customs	_____	_____
Lights out	_____	_____
Other:		_____

Session 2

ENCOURAGING
POSITIVE
BEHAVIOR

Chapter 4

EFFECTIVE DISCIPLINE AND ENCOURAGEMENT

he scene is the playground at Eastside Elementary School. Two boys are throwing a ball back and forth when a third boy, Steven, runs up and grabs the ball.

"Hey! We were playing with that!" shouts one of the boys indignantly.

"So what?" says Steven. "It's my turn."

"You can have it when we're through," says the other.

"Try to take it from me," taunts Steven.

"Okay," says the first boy as he lunges for the ball. Steven quickly moves the ball out of the way and trips the boy, knocking him down.

"Here, you can have your stupid ball!" shouts Steven as he throws the ball at his victim's head. It bounces off the side of the boy's face. Furious now, he gets up and tackles Steven. As the two roll on the ground fighting, the teacher, Ms. Green, hears the commotion and runs to the scene to break it up.

That night, Steven's mother is finishing the dishes when the phone rings.

"Hello, Mrs. Jones? This is Susan Green, Steven's teacher. I'm afraid I need to talk with you about Steven's behavior."

No parent wants to begin a conversation with his child's teacher like this. We all want our children to be "well behaved" and successful in school. We're just not always sure what that means. Does "well behaved" mean that a child sits quietly at her desk all day, doing exactly what she is told, never challenging a teacher's idea or otherwise asserting herself? Maybe it did once. But in today's world most teachers are aware that successful behavior means thinking independently and taking positive action. The passive child who never causes a bit of trouble may not be learning the skills that will lead to success in the world outside the classroom.

Nevertheless, schools are communities and must have a degree of order to function effectively. School discipline plans, rules and other expectations of appropriate behavior are necessary for everyone to have a safe and satisfying learning environment. The child who knows how to live within the rules, make responsible choices and work cooperatively with others will have a much better chance of succeeding than the child who doesn't. Although you cannot be there to make sure your child is behaving appropriately, what you teach him at home can make a significant difference in how he behaves at school.

Although you cannot be there to make sure your child is behaving appropriately, what you teach him at home can make a significant difference in how he behaves at school.

The parenting skills you'll learn in this chapter will help foster positive behavior both at school and at home. But even more importantly, they'll help you instill the qualities your child needs to thrive in our society—qualities such as **responsibility, cooperation, courage, self-esteem** and **problem-solving ability.**

Let's look at two things your children need from you in order to develop the qualities that lead to success in school and beyond.

- Encouragement
- Discipline

Encouragement

When we en-courage a child we give her courage. We strengthen her to meet the challenges that school and life offer. Courage, from the French *coeur* (heart), is the confidence a child needs to risk failure. Your child is under pressure from peers to do something she knows is wrong. Will she have the courage to risk their disapproval, or will she go along with the group? Your child is struggling to master a new math concept. Will she keep trying or give up?

Children with a solid base of courage have the confidence to risk failure and to persevere when the going gets rough. They recognize that mistakes are for learning, and that failures in life do not make the person a failure. They have the emotional muscle to resist peer pressure and maintain the courage of their convictions. These children keep learning and moving ahead. Ultimately, they will find success. It's no wonder that psychologist Rudolph Dreikurs once wrote that "Children need encouragement like plants need water."

What Does Discouragement Look Like?

Discouraged children are more likely to develop behavior problems at school—fights on the playground, classroom disruptions and other actions—that take away their opportunities to learn.

Because a discouraged child is not getting satisfaction from learning and school, he will often look for other areas in which he can succeed. This may mean sports or social activities. It may also mean misbehavior. Discouraged children are more likely to develop behavior problems at school—fights on the playground, classroom disruptions and other actions—that take away their opportunities to learn.

What sometimes appears to parents and teachers as a motivation problem is often a fear of failure.

As parents, half of becoming effective encouragers is to cut down on the times that we do the opposite—discourage our children. If encouragement is to "instill courage," then discouragement is to "remove courage." What sometimes appears to parents and teachers as a motivation problem is often a fear of failure. The discouraged child unconsciously reasons, "If I don't care, then I don't have to try, and if I don't try, I can't really fail. They can give me an F, but since I didn't try it doesn't really count."

Let's look at four of the most common ways parents discourage their children:

- Focusing on mistakes
- Personality attacks and perfectionism
- Negative expectations
- Overprotection

Focusing on Mistakes

Try an experiment. As you are reading this sentence, are you aware of the temperature around you? If you are, chances are that you are either too hot or too cold. It's doubtful you were thinking, "It sure is comfortable in here." We notice the exceptions to what we like and expect and tend to take the positive for granted.

Unfortunately, this same tendency creeps into our parenting. It is easy for us to walk into a child's room and ignore the neatly made bed, the straight bookshelves and the clothes that have been put away in the drawers. But we *do* notice the damp bath towel lying in a heap beside the bed. "Caroline," you say, "you forgot to hang up your towel after your bath again."

Taken by itself, there is nothing so terrible about this comment. (Although you could have left off the "again" at the end of the sentence.) However, if you are not also careful to comment upon the things she is doing well—especially the organization of her room, since the negative comment related to that—then soon she comes to think she does more wrong than right. Such discouragement leads to more mistakes and misbehavior, which produce more criticism from the parent and so on. Eventually, the negative cycle surfaces in the class-room.

Children certainly need to be corrected when they make mistakes or misbehave. Correction helps them know what to do differently next time. But they probably need to hear four to five times as much about what they do right to balance the effect our criticism may have on their courage and self-esteem.

Personality Attacks and Perfectionism

When criticism is aimed at a child's personality rather than her behavior, the effect is damaging, not helpful. When we call our chil-dren names, such as "lazy," "careless" or "stupid," we are attacking their self-esteem and courage at their core. Not to mention that such tactics usually backfire. After all, if you tell a child that he is lazy, then what should you expect in the future but lazy behavior? Instead, focus your comments on the problem behavior. Don't say "Why are you so lazy?"; say instead, "You haven't done your chores."

A subtle form of personality attack is perfectionism. This is the tendency always to require more from the child than she is giving. The message of perfectionism is that no matter how well you do, you should have done better. When children come to believe that they are never quite good enough, they lose motivation: "I never do it well enough anyway, so why try?"

Even when these children seem to keep trying, they never feel secure in their achievements. They may get all A's, but rather than enjoying the accomplishment, they are already worrying about the next challenge to their perfection. Such perfectionist thinking has been linked to eating disorders and depression in adolescents.

Negative Expectations

In a classic psychology experiment, teachers were told that half the students in their classes had tested high on a measure predicting academic success, and the other half had tested low. In fact, the students were randomly assigned to the two groups, regardless of academic abilities. At the end of the semester, guess which group had the better grades? The group the teachers thought would do better actually did do better. Conversely, the teachers' negative expectations for the other group was a significant factor in the group's poor showing. Negative expectations from teachers and parents discourage children from trying.

Negative expectations from teachers and parents discourage children from trying.

Our children can sense when we expect the worst from them, even if we don't use the words. If you believe your child is hopeless in math, you can say, "I know you can do this," but your tone of voice will give a different message. Or perhaps you wait only a few seconds for your child to answer a question and then hurriedly give him the answer. You and your child may not even be consciously aware of this difference, but the message is received: "You don't think I can get it."

Children must be free to overcome their frustrations, solve their own problems and accept the consequences of their choices if they are to develop the stamina required to succeed in school and in the community.

Overprotection

When we step in and do for children what they could eventually do for themselves, we send the message that "you can't handle it." While children should be protected in matters of health and safety, we are overprotecting when we are quick to rescue them from the reasonable problems and conflicts that come their way. Children must be free to overcome their frustrations, solve their own problems and accept the consequences of their choices if they are to develop the stamina required to succeed in school and in the community.

The overprotected child easily gives up when things are difficult. She is quick to shout "it's not fair" at the slightest transgression. She looks for someone else to solve her problems and lives with many unrealistic fears that hamper her growth. Her underlying belief becomes, "The world is dangerous and difficult, and I can't handle it myself."

Think of the problems such attitudes cause in the classroom, where teachers cope with 25 or more students and must rely on a degree of independence from each one. An overprotected child who expects special treatment at school is in for a frustrating, discouraging time.

How can a parent tell when she is offering reasonable protection and when she is overprotecting? Two rules of thumb may help:

1. **Ask yourself what is the worst that could happen if you don't step in.** If the answer is a serious threat to your child's well-being or safety, then interfere. For example, not wearing seat belts, a bike helmet or rollerblade gear could result in a serious injury. Going alone to the mall might lead to abduction or other victimization. Going to unsupervised parties could lead to the use of alcohol and other drugs or the dangerous effects of drug use, such as crime and violence.

   On the other hand, pulling your child out of soccer because she took a hard fall is overprotection. Worrying yourself sick because your son won't eat his vegetables is overprotection. Running to the school and demanding an explanation from your child's teacher because she disciplined him is overprotecting.

2. **Never do for your child on a regular basis what your child can do for herself.** If your child is seven or older, can she set an alarm clock and get herself up in the morning? Can your child put her own clothes in the hamper, or do you pick up after her? Do you ask her to help set the table for dinner and do other family chores?

   Be on guard against the rationalization, "But it's easier to do it myself." It may be easier and faster in the short run, but think of the damage you do in the long run. Eventually your child may not be able to do much of anything for himself, including school work, that presents a challenge.

Turning Discouragement into Encouragement

Avoiding the tendency to discourage our children is a major step in the right direction. The next step is to look for opportunities to actively encourage them. We can use the power of encouragement in general ways to build a bedrock of courage and self-esteem, and we can use it in specific ways to encourage positive behavior, values and attitudes.

Instead of...	We can...
focusing on mistakes	build on strengths
expecting too much—perfectionism	show acceptance
negative expectations	show confidence
expecting too little—overprotection	stimulate independence

Build on Strengths

The old saying, "nothing succeeds like success," sums up the benefit of focusing attention on what we do well. Our successes bolster our courage and motivate us to want to do even better. The same is true for our children. Helping them experience the joy of achievement and then commenting on the strengths they called upon to make achievement happen is a wonderful way to encourage further progress. Here are some keys to using this powerful form of encouragement:

1. **Focus your encouragement on the behavior rather than the child.**

   ### Example

   NO: *"You were a good boy at the restaurant tonight."*

   YES: *"I really appreciate the way you used your best manners at the restaurant tonight. It really made the evening more enjoyable."*

Parents sometimes ask what is wrong with telling a child that she is "a good girl," or otherwise praising her personality. Children experience such praise as a double-edged sword: "I am a 'good' girl when I do what you want; therefore, I must be a 'bad' girl when I don't."

2. **Comment on the effort, not just the results.**

> ### Example
>
> NO: *Not saying anything until grades come out at the end of the quarter.*
>
> YES: *Giving encouragement throughout the year: "You are really working hard on your reading. I can hear the improvement."*

3. **Break large tasks into smaller steps.**

> ### Examples
>
> NO: *"Let's organize your room today."*
>
> YES: *"Let's organize your closet today."*
>
> LATER: *"You did a great job with the closet! Doesn't it look terrific? How about making a date to tackle the bookshelf next?"*

4. **Look for past examples of strengths to encourage your child to take the next step.**

Example

NO: *"I know you can do this report."*

YES: *"You did a good job writing that paper on Eleanor Roosevelt. I know this report is a little longer, but I'll bet if you break it down into sections, you'll do a fine job."*

Show Acceptance

Parents who are achievers sometimes unwittingly send the message that they accept their children *as long as they perform to their parents' standards.* Because all children have a fundamental need to belong, to feel accepted and wanted—especially by their parents—any suspicion that Mom's or Dad's acceptance is conditional undermines children's sense of security, self-esteem and courage.

We must let our children know through our words and actions that we love and value them for themselves—just because they are our children. Our acceptance is free and unconditional. Sure, we want to encourage their success, and we do not accept certain behavior as okay, but we always accept them as unique and special human beings who are gifts in our lives.

"I really enjoy being with you."

"I can tell it's you from hearing that great laugh of yours."

"I know you're disappointed in not making the team, but you tried your best, and that's what's important."
"I'm glad you are my daughter."

Show Confidence

All children can learn, even though some may take longer than others to master a concept. Your confidence in your child's ability to keep going when he feels frustration and defeat, your confidence that he will eventually succeed, your confidence that he will make something useful of his life—this is the encouragement that can make the difference between success and failure.

To show confidence, you really have to believe that your child is capable of success. If you don't believe in her, then she has to overcome your doubts as well as her own. That's an uphill battle. Some tips:

1. **Keep your confidence in line with reality.** Just as it's silly to have confidence that you'll win the lottery, you don't want to set up false expectations by showing confidence that your son will make all A's when he has been struggling to pass.

Example

NO: *"I know you're failing this course, but I believe you can get an A if you really try."*

YES: *"I know you can pass this course if you will give it the same effort you give your rollerblading."*

2. **Show confidence by giving responsibility.** Allowing children to take on additional responsibilities is an excellent way to communicate your confidence. Keep the level of responsibility in line with their age and ability to handle it, then look for opportunities to encourage their efforts.

Examples

"We can get a pet hamster if you will feed it and clean out the cage."

"I think you are old enough to help me with some of the house chores. Would you rather start by learning how to use the vacuum cleaner or the furniture polish?"

3. **Ask your child's opinion.** This communicates that you have confidence in her ability to think.

Examples

"You've been studying about World War II. Do you think that was a war worth fighting?"

"Where do you think we should go on our picnic? The park or the nature center?"

4. **Don't rescue your children from frustration.** When children have difficulty with a task that we can easily do, it is very tempting to step in and take over. Instead, when they become

frustrated, try offering partial help and let them still take part of the credit. If you think they can complete the task by themselves if they keep trying, you might simply offer encouragement.

Examples

"You can do it. Keep at it."

"Come on, just a little more and you'll have it."

"Here, let me help you pull the bow through. Now, you pull it tight. Great!"

Stimulate Independence

As children learn to do more and more for themselves, they become more confident, take on new challenges, learn more and continue to succeed. By stimulating our children's independence, we can help them grow into mature, responsible adults.

Examples

"Now that we've gone over the steps in order, I think you can do this project on your own. I'm looking forward to seeing it when you're finished."

"From now on I'd like each of us to make his own bed before coming down for breakfast."

More Encouragement Tips

As you look for ways to encourage each of your children, keep in mind that what one child finds encouraging, another may find discouraging. Observe what words or actions each of your children best responds to. Make sure that you:

- **Make the encouragement immediate.** The sooner your encouragement follows the attitude or behavior you approve, the more powerful it is.

- **Make the encouragement genuine.** If you tell your child she is doing well when she knows she isn't, your credibility isn't worth much. Future encouragement may be doubted, even when it's sincere.

- **Make the encouragement specific.** Specific positive feedback tells your children what to keep doing in the future. This promotes both motivation and improvement: "I like the way you used gray in the sky. It makes the castle look more gloomy."

What Encouragement Sounds Like

You can use hundreds of words and phrases to actively encourage your children. Find the ones that suit your style and please your children's ears. Here are some ideas:

attagirl	awesome	way to go
nice job	I really like that	you can do it
now you're getting it	great	terrific
super	neat	cool
attaboy	amazing	thanks
I appreciate it	you got it	you made it
you did it	superb	wonderful
bingo	now you're cooking	keep it up
that's the way	I'm proud of you	you must feel proud
you really earned it	good for you	gimme five
wow!	good effort	nice try
try again, you can do it	how special!	very good

Discipline

The word discipline comes from the Latin *disciplina*, meaning instruction. Your child needs instruction in cooperative behavior just as he needs instruction in reading, writing and arithmetic. And as we have found over the years that teaching the three r's requires more thoughtful approaches than a smack with a ruler, we have also found that cooperation requires more thoughtful discipline than spanking or other forms of punishment. Providing encouragement for your child usually decreases the amount of discipline he needs. But remember that children are learning, and some discipline is still required. This is why parents who are overly permissive with their children often find themselves frustrated by uncooperative, unmotivated and disrespectful behavior.

As you think about your methods of discipline, remember that your goal is to instruct your child, not to hurt him. It is Dark-Age-thinking that says we must hurt children to teach them. When we resort to name calling, yelling and other attempts to hurt the child physically or emotionally, the child is likely to take these as personal attacks—and rebel. The parent most determined to crush rebellion is often the one who ends up locked in power struggles.

The parent most determined to crush rebellion is often the one who ends up locked in power struggles.

A good test for your discipline style is to think about how you would like to be treated when given a traffic ticket by a police officer or reprimanded by a supervisor in business. Chances are an attack on your character would build resentment, not improvement. Children who resent discipline are more likely to rebel against authority, at home and at school.

The goal of discipline is to influence our children to choose positive behavior and attitudes by making it less worth their while to choose negative ones. The key is to begin gently, becoming progressively firmer as necessary to achieve this goal. Though it is beyond the scope of this book to cover all effective modern discipline techniques, the ones we will present have proven particularly powerful. Three basic levels of discipline will cover most problems:

- Polite requests and reminders
- Firm directions
- Natural and logical consequences

Polite Requests and Reminders

Children's misbehavior is often a product of ignorance. They simply may not know exactly what is expected of them in a given situation. When we come down too hard on them, they may be initially startled, and then resentful. Whether or not they change their behavior, we have damaged the relationship. Since a positive relationship is needed to influence our children—not to mention needed for our own satisfaction as parents—we want to use the least force necessary to bring about change. Often a polite request or reminder is all that it takes.

Examples

"Jack, I noticed that you forgot to take your books up to your room."

"Sandra, would you help me out by taking your dirty dishes back to the sink when you are through with your snack?"

"Carl, it's 5:00. Time to begin your homework."

Firm Directions

Most of us have learned that a polite request from an authority figure is equivalent to an order. It just feels better to be asked than told. However, if your child does not respond to a gentle nudge, increase the power by telling him what to do while using a firmer tone of voice. Do this *before* you get angry, as anger often produces a harsh, aggressive tone of voice that tempts some children into rebelling. Stay calm and firm.

Examples

"Jack, please take your books up to your room right now."

"Sandra, I've already asked you to take your dishes to the sink. Please stop what you are doing and do it now."

"Carl, turn off the video game until after you have done your homework."

If your child procrastinates, you can increase the demand by getting firmer and shorter in your communication.

Examples

"Jack, now!"

"Sandra, go!"

"Carl, homework!"

If your child still ignores your requests or if you're not comfortable with a firmer command, move to the third level of discipline, natural and logical consequences.

Natural and Logical Consequences

To be effective, consequences should be viewed by children as the logical extension of their choices, rather than arbitrary punishments imposed by parents or teachers.

Children learn responsibility by seeing that how they choose to behave leads to certain results, or consequences. You can use this idea of consequences for actions as a discipline tool. To be effective, however, consequences should be viewed by children as the logical extension of their choices, rather than arbitrary punishments imposed by parents or teachers. Let's look at the two types of consequences and how they teach.

Natural Consequences

These result naturally from a child's behavior, without the intervention of a parent or teacher. You might say that Mother Nature supplies this type of consequence.

Examples

The natural consequence of leaving a jacket at a friend's house is not having the jacket to wear the next time the child needs it.

The natural consequence of not eating breakfast is getting hungry before lunch.

Natural consequences work well because they allow the parent to be a sympathetic third party rather than a disciplinarian. There are, however, situations in which you do *not* want to allow the natural consequences to do the teaching:

1. **When the natural consequences are too dangerous.** For example, the natural consequence of playing with fire might be catching the house on fire, or worse.

2. **When the natural consequences are so far in the future that the child does not realize the connection.** For example, the natural consequence of not keeping up with schoolwork might be limited employment and postsecondary school options.

3. **When the natural consequences of the child's behavior affect someone other than the child.** For example, the child borrows your hammer and loses it.

In these and other situations parents can step in and use *logical* consequences.

Logical Consequences

Logical consequences are results that a parent or other authority figure provides to teach children what logically follows when they violate family rules or the needs of the situation.

Examples

A logical consequence for not finishing homework might be using Saturday free time to complete the assignment.

A logical consequence for throwing a bat in a baseball game might be calling the batter out.

An effective logical consequence will be one that your child cares about and that fits logically with the misbehavior you are trying to change. This is the principal difference between logical consequences and punishment: Punishment is an arbitrary reaction to a misbehavior that is not connected directly to the misbehavior itself. Taking away television privileges because a child did not brush her teeth is punishment. What is the connection or logic between not brushing teeth and television? There is none. Logical consequences, on the other hand, provide this connection. Use the following guidelines to create your logical consequence:

Punishment is an arbitrary reaction to a misbehavior that is not connected directly to the misbehavior itself.

1. Give the child a choice.
2. Ask the child to help set the consequences.
3. Make sure the consequences are really logical.
4. Only give choices that you can live with.
5. Keep your tone of voice firm and calm.

6. Give the choice one time, then act.

7. Expect the child to test you.

8. Allow the child to try again.

Let's take a closer look at each one.

1. Give the child a choice. In order for your child to learn responsibility, he must perceive some degree of choice. If you dictate to him, his only choice becomes to do what you say or rebel. If you give him  a choice, on the other hand, you have empowered him, shifted the responsibility to him and allowed him to save face. Two types of choices work well:

■ **either/or choices**

> ### Examples
>
> *"**Either** finish your homework **or** you'll do it during free time on Saturday."*
>
> *"**Either** hold on to your bat when you swing **or** you will be called out."*

■ **when/then choices**

Examples

*"**When** you have taken your bath, **then** you may continue working on the puzzle."* (This "work before play" philosophy helps children set positive priorities and gives you a powerful logical consequence to use in many situations.)

*"**When** you have finished your report, **then** you may make your phone call."*

*"**When** you have brushed your teeth, **then** I will read a story to you if there is still time."* (Use this kind of example if you have a set bedtime routine in which a story regularly follows all chores. In this case, the logical consequence is different from a reward because the positive outcome is part of a normal routine and therefore not a bribe. Using rewards becomes counterproductive, as your child will begin expecting the reward or payoff every time. If your child misses the reading time, make sure you make up this important activity the next day.)

Be careful when giving choices to phrase them positively. If you use them as threats ("If you don't take your bath, then you can't work on the puzzle"), your child will see them as punishment and be more likely to rebel.

2. **Ask the child to help set the consequences.** Inviting children to help create the consequences not only reduces power struggles (you are giving them some power), it also helps teach the valuable skill of problem solving. Explain the problem to your child and calmly ask for his input in finding a solution.

Example

"Running into the street is dangerous. You might get hit by a car. What do you think we can do to help you remember to stay in the yard?"

Children may at first shrug and say "I don't know" when invited to come up with solutions. That's okay. The invitation itself is encouraging. Once they have had some experience with logical consequences, you'll be amazed at how helpful some of their suggestions will be. Of course, you always want to have your own logical consequence in mind, in case you aren't comfortable with the one your child comes up with.

3. **Make sure the consequences are really logical.** The challenge in learning to use logical consequences is to train ourselves to think logically. This means continually envisioning different logical results for different situations. Punishment is easier, because one punishment can be used to fit any misbehavior. Maybe that's why children resent it and tend to rebel even more. As you practice using logical consequences and talk with other parents who use them, you'll find it easier and easier to come up with logically related consequences.

4. **Only give choices that you can live with.** When you give your child a choice, you must be prepared to tolerate whichever option she selects, even if it's not the one you hoped she would choose. Be sure you can calmly accept and live with the consequence you have agreed to.

Example

"Either play in the yard and out of the street, or come into the kitchen and sit with me while I get dinner ready."

Don't use this logical consequence if you know that having this child in the kitchen while you prepare dinner is going to drive you crazy. Think of something you can live with.

Example

"Either play in the yard and out of the street, or play in your room until dinner is ready."

Remember, you are the leader. You don't have to agree to something you don't believe in.

A logical consequence can easily turn into punishment when a parent's tone of voice and body language communicate an angry attempt to coerce a child into changing behavior.

5. **Keep your tone of voice firm and calm.** Getting angry often not only devalues your anger, it also invites power struggles. A logical consequence can easily turn into punishment when a parent's tone of voice and body language communicate an angry attempt to coerce a child into changing behavior. Kids who are prone to anger and confrontation themselves often take parents' angry tone as a challenge. This triggers their rebellious side, and the result is a frustrating struggle for power. A calm and firm tone, however, communicates that you are a powerful leader who means business. You are not going to be ruffled by a misbehaving child.

    Note: Sometimes anger is called for. When your children are risking their safety or someone else's, for example, your anger might cue them to how serious you think the situation is. This is likely to be effective only if they rarely see you angry.

One of the most frequent discipline mistakes that parents make is to talk too much and act too little.

6. **Give the choice one time, then act.** One of the most frequent discipline mistakes that parents make is to talk too much and act too little. If you keep giving the same choice over and over without applying the logical consequence, your child learns to push you to the limit. Instead, give the choice one time.

Example

"Susan, you can either get into the bathtub right now or go straight to bed. You've got until 'five' to decide. One...two...three...four...four and a half...five."

Wait a moment for your child to make her decision. What if she doesn't say what her decision is? Watch her behavior. Children communicate their choices through their behavior. If your child procrastinates, use a timer or count to five to let her clearly know what the limits are and when the logical consequence will go into effect.

7. **Expect your child to test you.** Children may continue to misbehave as a way of testing this new approach to discipline. Expect this challenge, and you'll be less likely to get discouraged when the misbehavior continues for a while. If you follow through with the logical consequence, if you refuse to fight or give in and if you are consistent in this approach, children will usually respond with positive behavior. If the behavior does not improve after several applications of the logical consequence, check to see if you are following the guidelines. If you are, begin again with a new logical consequence that may have more importance to your child.

8. **Allow the child to try again.** Since the purpose of discipline is to instruct, we want our children to learn from the experience.

Therefore, you want to give your child a chance to make a better choice next time and to experience the desired consequence. If your child continues to choose misbehavior, increase the amount of time before he is allowed to choose again.

Examples

"Shandra, it isn't fun to play with you when you don't play fairly. Either play the game by the rules, or we will have to put the game away for today."

The next time Shandra plays unfairly, the parent can say:

"I see you've chosen not to play anymore today. We can try again tomorrow."

If Shandra continues to play unfairly the next day, the parent might say:

"Shandra, maybe we need to put the game away for a few days. We can try again this weekend."

Using logical consequences and the other discipline methods discussed here will help you provide the guidance your child needs to behave appropriately at home and at school. Learning that there are consequences to misbehavior at home will provide the reasonable expectation that there will be consequences for misbehavior at school. *The child who learns that he can get away with outlandish or disrespectful behavior at home will expect to get away with it at school.*

Discipline will rarely work if the child's positive efforts are ignored.

These eight guidelines will help make logical consequences a powerful form of discipline. Remember, though, that discipline will rarely work if the child's positive efforts are ignored.
ENCOURAGE!

Causes of Classroom Misbehavior

If you are providing the kinds of encouragement and discipline that inspire positive behavior and are still getting reports of trouble at school, you may need to look into other causes of misbehavior. The following list of possible causes may help you pinpoint the difficulty. Chapter references that follow each item direct you to helpful information.

- **improper nutrition** (causes low energy or lack of attention or participation; see Chapter 2)

- **physical problems, such as poor vision or hearing** (see Chapter 2)

- **a specific learning disability** (see Chapters 3, 7 and 8)

- **family problems, such as divorcing parents** (see Chapter 3)

- **difficulty mastering the material being taught** (see Chapters 7 and 8)

- **repeated clashes with a teacher** (see Chapter 3)

- **problems with other students, such as bullying or peer pressure** (see Chapter 1)

- **poor attitude toward school or teacher** (see Chapter 5)

Chapter 5

ATTITUDES THAT BUILD SUCCESS

I know a neurosurgeon who jokes about giving his children an "attitude adjustment." If only teaching positive attitudes were as easy as flipping the right switches in the brain. For better or worse, the formation of attitudes is not an absolute science. A very strong attitude may arise in a single moment of intense emotional experience, such as a trauma, or it may evolve slowly from a combination of events experienced and interpreted by the child. Many of our core attitudes develop at an unconscious level; unless we look deeply, we may never identify these hidden decisions that govern our emotions and behavior.

The good news is that attitudes can change. As existentialist Jean-Paul Sartre expressed it, the unique thing about being human is that at any moment in your life, you can make a decision that changes the rest of your life. Helping your children choose positive attitudes is an ongoing (and rewarding) opportunity for parents.

What is your child's attitude toward school? Does he enjoy learning? Does he respect school rules? Does he respect the teacher? Does he think it's worthwhile to stick with tough assignments? Does he like working with other students? These and other attitudes govern your child's behavior and influence it in positive or negative directions.

Just as it is important for you to influence your child's behavior towards success, you also want to influence her attitudes and beliefs in ways that

will lead to success. We will look first at specific beliefs that are
known to build success and then at methods you can use to help instill
these beliefs (or any others) in your children.

Beliefs that Build Success

"I am capable of learning."

Children who have trouble succeeding in school often develop a belief
that they cannot learn, no matter how hard they might try. "I don't get
it," becomes their slogan of defeat as they, their teachers and often their
parents gradually give up on them.

Wise parents and teachers know that these children *can* learn, and,
indeed, that all children have an innate desire and capacity to learn.
When parents convey this message by encouraging words and by
actions—such as breaking tasks into small, manageable parts the child
can handle—the child's success encourages him to take the next step.
When parents and teachers refuse to accept "I can't" and help students
change those words into "This is difficult, but I can get it if I stick with
it," children begin to believe they can learn. (See *How to Develop Self-
Esteem in Your Child: 6 Vital Ingredients*, by Bettie B. Youngs, Ph.D.,
Ed.D., Faucette, 1993, for more on the empowering effects of
self-esteem.)

"Learning is important to me."

A child who understands the value of learning is more likely to study,
complete homework and participate fully in school than one who thinks
it's all a waste of time. Why should learning be important to a child
when so many other activities bring more immediate pleasure?
Although adults realize that learning creates job and career opportunities, children are not capable of connecting work now with results so far

in the future. For a child to understand that learning is important, he must be able to see immediate gains. How can we influence children to believe that learning is important?

"Learning is fun."

We are all born wanting to know. Help to stimulate the natural curiosity in your child by focusing on the enjoyable process of learning rather than the end result of grades.

Example

"I'm happy to see that you enjoy camping so much, Emily. You've really learned a lot about marking trails."

Do not miss the many opportunities to marvel at your child's mastery of concepts and activities. Ironically, this outlook on school work will also help children make better grades and achieve more success. When learning is no longer tied to a tangible payoff, children who enjoy learning itself will continue to put forth effort even when the results are slow to come. (For more on making learning an enjoyable challenge, see Chapters 6, 7 and 8.)

"Learning is power."

When your child has mastered a concept or task, she feels a sense of power that translates into high self-esteem. This positive feeling is enhanced by the encouragement and praise of those she values. The four-year-old who learns to tie her shoes is proud of this new power she has over his environment. Her pride increases as her parents and teachers add their encouragement: "That's great! Look what you can do!" As your child gets older, continue to be amazed and impressed with her learning. Your interest and enthusiasm will help her want to learn more.

"Learning is important in my family."

Make learning a priority in your family. Show a genuine interest in what your child is learning. Take family field trips that make learning fun, such as to museums, zoos, libraries and nature centers.

Note: If you have a child whom people are always telling is "so pretty" or "so cute," be sure to add a compliment of your own about her learning ability. A very successful and attractive woman once said that she attributed her success in part to the fact that whenever someone would tell her mother in front of her how pretty she was, her mother would add, "And smart as a whip too!" She learned that looks were not enough—that learning and doing well in school were valued in her family.

"I learn from my mistakes."

Learning and making mistakes go hand in hand. Once children have mastered a new pursuit, they will make mistakes less often. But to move on to new learning means making more mistakes, and the only way to stop the process is to stop learning.

The child who is unusually afraid of mistakes probably sees them as evidence that something is wrong with him instead of as learning opportunities. This child loses out in one of two ways: Either he protects his self-esteem by avoiding new tasks and sticking to what he can already do well, or he ignores his mistakes, getting away from the pain as soon as he can and losing the opportunity to learn.

Helping your child be less afraid of her mistakes will give her permission to make them. If you or your child tends to be a perfectionist, this attitude is especially important. The belief that any mistake is bad undermines the courage to try and leads to frustration and hostility. For high achievers, it is better to shift your goal from the unrealistic one of perfection to that of mastery. To get there, make a learning exercise out of identifying mistakes.

Example

"Let's look at this problem that your teacher marked wrong on your math assignment and see if we can figure out why you put that answer."

Adopting a matter-of-fact tone may help convince your child that you see this as an interesting process rather than a chance to assign blame.

On the other hand, if your child seems indifferent to his mistakes, slow him down and point out where he went wrong. Let him know that by correcting the mistake, he will learn what to do differently next time. Help him to see that concentration can eliminate many careless errors.

Example

"Read that paragraph again, slowly, and tell me if you think it makes sense."

"I am an achiever."

Children who see themselves as achievers usually accomplish more than those who see themselves as failures or as lucky to get by. They set goals for themselves, and they work to achieve those goals. They tend to plan better, schedule their time and follow through with study and assignments. You can help supply this achievement motivation, as it's called, by teaching your child to set goals, then working with her to determine the many small steps necessary to achieving each goal.

Example

"I know this seems like a big report, but you've got two weeks to do it. Let's break it down into small steps and take them one at a time."

Encourage effort along the way, and celebrate together as each step is completed.

Examples

"Hey! This outline looks great. What's on the schedule for tonight? Writing the introduction?"

"Great job! All done on time. You deserve a lot of credit."

One word of caution: Some people develop too much of a taste for achievement and find that they are never quite satisfied. They sacrifice the joy of learning to achievement at all costs. If this description fits you or your child, try sometimes to shift your focus from the end result to the process.

Example

"The casserole wasn't as delicious as I thought it would be, but I'm glad we tried that new recipe."

"I am a problem solver."

The successful student, like the successful adult, is not one whose life is free from problems, but one who has learned that he can solve his problems effectively. This belief helps him to accept new challenges with confidence, knowing that he will find solutions as problems arise.

To help, parents can avoid the temptation to step in and take over when their children are stumped. Use your encouragement skills to show confidence in your child's ability to find a solution, offering as little guidance as necessary to help. "Do you want a hint?" is a much better way to help than "Here, let me show you . . . ." Often, just letting your child work on the problem alone for a little while is your best bet.

When your family runs into problems, you can model problem-solving skills by looking for solutions together: "Who has an idea that might work?" (See *Problem Solving Skills for Children*, by Bettie B. Youngs, Ph.D., Ed.D., Jalmar Press, 1992, for more on this topic.)

"I want to cooperate with others."

The world is full of adults who had no trouble learning in school (at least, learning academics), but who were still unsuccessful at school— and in life—because they never learned to get along with others. The

ability to work cooperatively with both peers and those in authority is an essential element of success.

Believing in the value of cooperation will help your child make the compromises necessary for getting along with others. Taking turns, sharing and listening to other's opinions do not come easily for children. These actions must be learned and relearned. You can help by looking for chances to point out why cooperation is important.

Example

"Jill is still talking, Michael. Let's let her finish, then you can tell us what you think. That way we won't miss any good ideas."

Playing together offers many opportunities for you to talk about cooperative behavior and show your appreciation for the times your child exhibits this behavior.

Example

"You showed good sportsmanship back there when you called that foul on yourself. Thanks."

Talk to your child about the needs of others and about differences among people of varying cultures, ages and personalities. Then compliment her when she helps others or shows respect for their differences.

"I will play within the rules."

Just as an athlete would have little chance of success in a sporting event if he played outside the rules, a child cannot thrive in school if he is constantly breaking the rules. Successful students recognize this fact and make the decision to follow the school's rules.

Enlightened older students go one step further and recognize that the only way for a large group to function efficiently is to establish rules, and that it is in the group members' best interest to support those rules.

You can help your child develop this belief by understanding and supporting the school's rules yourself. Talk with your child about the teacher's or the school discipline plan (see Know and Support the School's Discipline Plan, from Chapter 3) and about why it's important for all students to play within these rules. You might use the sports analogy to help your child appreciate how ludicrous organized events would be if everyone made up their own rules. Finally, you can use a combination of encouragement and discipline skills (see Chapter 4) to help influence your child to accept limits at home and at school.

"My teacher is the authority in this classroom."

The days when a teacher commanded unquestioned respect from his students—usually to the tune of the hickory stick—have gone the way of the slide rule. Most educators today realize that respect must be mutual between teacher and student, and that children have a right to be treated with dignity and respect in school.

Unfortunately, the pendulum of change has, for many students, swung too far the other way, and disrespect for the teacher prevails in many modern classrooms. When this happens, it is the students—and their parents—who suffer most. When a student has no respect for her teacher's ability, she is more likely to be inattentive, unproductive, unmotivated and prone to troublemaking. Under these conditions, is it any wonder that she has a hard time translating her abilities and intelligence into school success?

Perceptive children are often good at detecting a teacher's shortcomings. Older children especially may take it upon themselves to decide that the teacher is not qualified. Parents can help such children by focusing on what this teacher has to offer instead of what he lacks.

"I'm sorry you don't think Mr. Henderson makes his lectures very interesting. I certainly was impressed at the open house with all the interesting science projects he's planned for this year. Maybe you could concentrate on taking really good notes on the lectures—it might make them seem more interesting."

It is very important for parents to guard against putting down a child's teacher.

It is very important for parents to guard against putting down a child's teacher. A negative word by a parent can give a child the impression that he does not have to respect his teacher. Imagine how infuriated you would be if a teacher were to undermine you by telling your child you were not a very good parent. If you have serious concerns about a teacher's abilities, make an appointment to talk with the teacher. Use the cooperative problem-solving model described in Chapter 3 to try to resolve the situation. If this fails, talk with the principal. *But do not join in a conspiracy with your child.* This only makes it more difficult for your child to treat his teacher with the respect all teachers deserve.

"My choices matter."

Responsibility means accepting that what happens to us results from the choices we make.

Your children need to believe that their choices do matter, because they lead to consequences that affect themselves and others. The student who chooses to play within the rules at school, keep up with her assignments, study hard and cooperate with peers and teachers will do better than she would if she chose the opposite. Responsibility means accepting that what happens to us results from the choices we make. You can help your child learn responsibility by looking for opportunities to give choices, then allowing her to experience the consequences of those choices.

> ### Example
>
> *"Would you help me plan the menu for this week? But remember that you didn't feel so good after you ate so much cheese yesterday? What do you think we could substitute?"*

Even young children can be given simple either/or choices.

> ### Example
>
> *"Would you rather have cold cereal or oatmeal this morning?"*

You can also help your child learn to make better choices by encouraging him to predict the possible consequences of his choices.

> ### Examples
>
> *"What might happen if you tried that?"*
>
> *"What else could you do?"*

In Chapter 4 we discussed how choices can be combined with consequences in a discipline technique called logical consequences. This method is not only effective at correcting misbehavior, it is also a terrific way of teaching your children that their choices matter.

"I am responsible for my success."

Children who believe they are responsible for their own success have what is called an internal locus of control. They see themselves in control of their destiny and able to change events when they are going poorly. Children with an external locus of control, on the other hand, see others as in charge of their lives. They often have very little hope of improving their situations. Research shows that children with an internal locus of control are more effective in school and elsewhere than those who blame others and make excuses for their results. Many people have overcome poor home and school situations because they accepted the responsibility—and opportunity—of shaping their own destiny.

Research shows that children with an internal locus of control are more effective in school and elsewhere than those who blame others and make excuses for their results.

To help your child believe she is the master of her fate, avoid taking over her responsibilities yourself. This means limiting your involvement to a support role and not overprotecting or doing your child's work for her.

Example

"Homework is your responsibility, and I know you can handle it. How can I help?"

Give her full credit for her successes and responsibility for her mistakes.

Example

"I know you don't think the test was fair, but what can you learn from the situation that might help you better prepare for the next one?"

Chapter 4 has more on stimulating independence and avoiding overprotection.

"I honor my commitments."

Keeping one's agreements is an important ingredient in living success-fully. First, our credibility depends on it. Second, the effort we expend to honor our commitments comes back to us in the form of high self-esteem. Children feel good about themselves when they are keeping up with their work and doing a good job. Their satisfaction and sense of power build a strong foundation for future achievement.

You can help by pointing out your child's commitments whenever he seems to forget them. The child who puts off his weekend homework until Sunday night and then wants to watch a TV program can be reminded that schoolwork is his first obligation. The child who has signed up for a soccer team but wants to miss a game because she's been invited to a friend's house can be reminded of her responsibility to the team. Parental encouragement is usually enough to help such children put their priorities in order and do the right thing. If this fails, you may need to call upon logical consequences and other respectful forms of discipline.

"My fears won't stop me."

Because learning is so filled with mistakes and setbacks, your child's ability to thrive in school requires the courage to risk failure regularly in order to succeed. You can help by encouraging your child when she is afraid of a new challenge. Perhaps she is petrified of giving a book report in front of the class. You might encourage her by having her practice in front of you while you smile, nod and offer specific praise for sections you particularly like. Your child may want to try out for a speaking part in the school pageant, yet he's afraid he won't be chosen. Help him to see that having the courage to try out gives him at least a chance at getting the part, a chance he wouldn't have if he gave in to his fears and avoided the challenge.

If your child appears truly afraid of something, help her evaluate the risks in the situation. Does the challenge present a serious threat to her health or safety? If so, you might support her in avoiding that risk. But if the risk is one of ego, you can help her understand the lessons taught by the many famous men and women throughout history who overcame fear and failure to succeed. Keep an eye out for books, videos and stories about people who showed perseverance in the face of obstacles. Older children might enjoy reading John F. Kennedy's *Profiles in Courage*. You might want to retell these stories to your children at bedtime.

"When the work is difficult I stick with it."

We talked about courage as a willingness to overcome fear and risk failure. Perhaps equally important for school success is the courage to tolerate frustration. In fact, the two are closely related. When a child becomes frustrated with a task, chances are he has run into a temporary series of small failures. "I tried this and it didn't work. So I tried that and it didn't work either. Then I tried this and struck out again." When learning does not come easily, some children are quick to become frustrated, get upset and eventually give up.

Thomas Edison reportedly tried more than 2,000 filaments for the electric light bulb before finding one that worked. Most successful entrepreneurs report that they didn't get to where they are by being the smartest or most creative people around, but by persisting when others would have lost heart and given up.

You can help your child adopt the same belief by offering encouragement when she becomes frustrated. Remind her of past successes and what it took to achieve them.

> ### Example
>
> *"Remember how hard you had to practice basketball before you made the team? Planning this project is really no different."*

Note: Sometimes frustration means that a child really does need additional help with academics. If you suspect your child needs outside help with school work, consult the teacher to see if tutoring or other special assistance is in order.

How to "Teach" a Positive Belief

Talk about the Belief with Your Child

Look for opportunities to talk about beliefs with your child. Discuss why you think a particular belief is important and look for agreement from your child. Ask him to tell you why he thinks it is important and look for chances to agree with him.

You and your child might make a poster listing positive beliefs. Hang it where she'll see it regularly, perhaps where she does her homework. You could even create a separate poster for each belief, or create a notebook with a separate section for each belief. Then, over the coming months, together collect evidence that your child supports this belief. For example, under "I am an achiever," you might include successfully completed school papers or a photo of your child attaining one of her goals, such as receiving a badge in scouts.

When watching TV or a movie together, be on the alert for stories in which having a positive belief led to success, or not having it caused problems. Ask your children afterwards what messages they got from the story. Don't turn the discussion into a sermon or criticism session. Instead, keep the conversation focused on the characters in the story and how their attitudes and behaviors led to their consequences. Your child will learn your attitudes from how you judge these characters without the pain of direct confrontation. Reading fables and other poignant stories aloud can also provide a good starting point for such a discussion.

"Walk Your Talk"

Talking about our beliefs with our children is a good first step. But as someone once said, if you want to know what a person really believes, do not listen to the tongue in his mouth; watch the tongue in his shoe. It's his behavior that will give him away.

If you tell your child that cooperation is important, do you then take pains not to interrupt her when she's talking? If you tell your child that learning is important, do you drive the message home by learning new skills or even reading a book instead of watching TV every night? These are much more powerful messages about what you value than words alone. And by setting good examples for our children, we get back in touch with the best aspects of ourselves. This self-enrichment is an unexpected pay-off, as we work to improve our credibility with our children.

Walk Your Talk

DO	DON'T
keep learning	choose only recreation and entertainment
read	watch too much TV
learn from your mistakes	be harshly self-critical
set goals, keep striving	give up, become complacent
show respect for authority by obeying the law	try to get away with "minor" infringements, such as speeding
share decision-making	dictate or abdicate
listen to your children	interrupt
keep your agreements	forget or ignore your agreements
accept responsibility for your actions	blame and make excuses
make time for your family	overvalue lesser priorities
take reasonable risks	play it too safe or too recklessly
tolerate frustration	give up or become upset

Show Up at School

It is difficult for your children to believe school is really important if they don't think it's important to you.

This particular way to "walk your talk" deserves special emphasis. It is difficult for your children to believe school is really important if they don't think it's important to you. Being there for parent meetings, conferences, your children's special events and other opportunities sends a clear message that this is important—important enough for you to go to the trouble of making arrangements to be there. Obviously, there are times when legitimate circumstances will prevent you from participating. You can still show your interest. Ask your mate or a friend what happened at a program that you missed.

Those parents who have the time can go one step further. Most schools now have parent volunteer programs in which parents work in the library or the office, head up special projects or work in other capacities for a few hours a week. Many schools now train parents to be tutors. Some parent-teacher organizations offer volunteer opportunities that can be done at home in the evenings (such as making phone calls). Call your own school office to find out what needs the school has. Not only will you be helping to create a better school for everyone, you will also be instilling in your children the importance of education.

Encourage Positive Attitudes and Beliefs

Review the beliefs discussed in this chapter from time to time so they will remain fresh in your mind and then look for opportunities to catch your child expressing the belief, either in words or actions. Make encouraging comments to acknowledge the positive attitude.

For example, you notice that your son is having a difficult time getting started on a project. He asks you for some help. You go over the instructions with him, express confidence that he will think of a good way to proceed, then you leave. You come back 20 minutes later to check on his progress and see that he is working on the project. "What did you come up with?" you ask. After he explains, you say, "Great idea. I like the way you took responsibility for coming up with your own project, and that you didn't give up when it got difficult. I'll check back with you later."

Gently Confront Negative Beliefs

When we hear negative attitudes from our children, it is important to stay calm and not become discouraged ourselves. We want to avoid escalating the situation by blaming, criticizing or otherwise attacking our children's self-esteem. Suppose your child becomes frustrated while working on his science project. You see him staring at the ceiling and complaining that "I can't do it." What do you do? Here's a chance to gently attack the negative belief itself—and not your child's personality. Let's look at an example of such a situation:

Child: *"I can't do this! It's too hard."*

Parent: *"You sound really frustrated with this assignment."*

Child: *"Yeah. I don't even understand what she wants us to do."*

Parent: *"Sometimes difficult assignments take a while to figure out."*

Child: *"But I just don't get it. I'm not very good in science anyway."*

Parent: *"Let's stop right here for a minute. Who says you're not very good in science? Your teacher?"*

Child: *"Well, no."*

Parent: *"The other kids?"*

Child: *"No."*

Parent: *"Anybody?"*

Child: *"No, but I just don't get it."*

Parent: *"Do you mean that you don't get science in general, or just this assignment? As I recall, you've told me a lot of interesting things you've learned in science this year."*

Child: *"Well, I guess it's just this assignment, but I can't do it."*

Parent: *"So you're pretty good in science, but this project is hard for you. Is that it?"*

Child: *"Yeah. Real hard."*

Parent: *"And hard things take a little longer, don't they?"*

Child: *"Yeah, I guess."*

Parent: *"Well, you're usually good at sticking with it when things get tough. You usually come up with a solution."*

Child: *"I know."*

Parent: *"Do you want me to go over the instructions with you, or do you want to stick with this by yourself?"*

Child: *"I'll try some more. But if I still don't get it, will you help?"*

Parent: *"Sure. I'll be back in 15 minutes to see how you're doing. Don't worry. You'll get this assignment done. It's just going to take some time."*

This parent began by trying to understand what her child was feeling about the assignment. By identifying his feeling of frustration, she was able to empathize with him and establish a positive climate for helping. Next, she suggested a positive attitude that would help him succeed when she said that "difficult tasks sometimes take a little longer."

When the child slipped into a negative belief, she gently attacked the belief by asking for evidence. By doing so, she helped him realize that there was very little, if any, evidence to support the belief that he was not good at science. All this was done in a friendly, supportive tone as the mother tried to help her son see the mistakes in his thinking.

Finally, she offered to help him understand the assignment if he needed it. This was not an offer to do the assignment for him, or even with him. Rather, it was limited support to help him get going on his own.

Helping your children develop these positive attitudes will not only help them succeed in school, it will also help them find success and satisfaction in their work, their relationships and other important aspects of life.

BUILDING ON STRENGTHS

The key to encouragement is learning to recognize our own strengths and those of others. To help you recognize some of these strengths in yourself, your child and your partner (choose a friend if you are single), fill in the blanks below.

One thing I am good at doing is _____.

One thing my child is good at is _____.

One thing my partner is good at is _____.

One thing people like about me is _____.

One thing people like about my child is _____.

One thing people like about my partner is _____.

One thing I am learning to do is _____.

One thing that my child is learning to do is _____.

One thing that my partner is learning to do is _____.

One way I contribute to my family is _____.

One way my child contributes to our family is _____.

One way my partner contributes to our family is _____.

One quality that I like about myself is _____.

One quality that I like about my child is _____.

One quality that I like about my partner is _____.

LOGICAL CONSEQUENCES GUIDE SHEET

Think about an ongoing problem that you have with one of your children, a problem that has not improved with polite requests or firm directions.

What is the problem? _____

What would you like your child to do? _____

_____

_____

List two or three logical consequences that might be effective in influencing him to change his behavior:

For example: **Either** *ride your bike in the driveway* **or** *come in the house to play.*

For example: **When** *you have completed your homework,* **then** *you may play on the computer.*

Either _____ or _____

Either _____ or _____

When _____ then _____

When _____ then _____

Choose the logical consequence that you think will work best, then meet with your child to discuss the problem. If she is unable to come up with a logical consequence that you can live with, use the one you have just developed.

Be sure to encourage your child's positive effort.

ATTITUDE CHECKLIST

Each week, focus on one of the positive attitudes below. Talk about this attitude with your children. Look for ways to encourage this attitude throughout the week, and note these here.

Week	Positive attitude	Did I talk with my children? (check)	Ways to instill this attitude
Week 1	**Learning**		
	I can learn.	_____	_____
	Learning is important.	_____	_____
Week 2	**Achieving**		
	I am an achiever.	_____	_____
	I am a problem solver.	_____	_____
Week 3	**Cooperation**		
	I want to cooperate with others.	_____	_____
	I play within the rules.	_____	_____
	My teacher is in charge of this classroom.	_____	_____
Week 4	**Responsibility**		
	My choices matter.	_____	_____
	I am responsible for my success.	_____	_____
	I can be counted on.	_____	_____
Week 5	**Courage**		
	My fears won't stop me.	_____	_____
	When the work is hard, I stick with it.	_____	_____

Session 3

REINFORCING YOUR CHILD'S ACADEMIC SKILLS

Chapter 6

Imagine your child going to a job interview 15 or 20 years from now. What skills will be important for success in that new world? Although we can't predict the future, it's a pretty safe bet that many jobs—and the skills required for them—will be different than they are today. One of the reasons is computer technology. Educators are now faced with the challenge of machines that can store and instantly "remember" most of the learning that has traditionally occupied kids' time in school—math equations, dates, scientific data, spelling and grammar rules, to name a few. In fact, it begins to look as if one of our greatest challenges as parents and teachers is to equip our children to remain smarter than the machines!

So, what should learning be all about? Should children spend all their time on things like long division and spelling rules? Or should schools throw out the entire curriculum for something new? As usual, the most sensible answer lies somewhere in the middle. Children need to master basic skills of reading, writing and math. Otherwise they will lack the foundations for communicating with other people—or with the computer—and the ability to reason about important ideas and practical situations. They may still need some practice in memorizing interesting or basic material (such as fine poetry or the multiplication tables), and they will still profit by mastering rule systems for spelling, grammar and science.

However, research tells us clearly that "rote-level" learning (memorize, take the test, forget) does not stimulate the growth of intelligence as much as does "conceptual" learning (understand, see relationships with other learning, build on a foundation of meaning). Moreover, the human brain is capable of much more advanced skills than even the most complex computer. Future employers probably won't ask a prospective employee to recite the names of the kings of England; they will be far more interested in a different set of abilities:

- to be a highly motivated "self-starter"

- to solve new types of problems

- to come up with original ideas

- to communicate effectively—orally or in writing

- to work well in groups

- to analyze, organize and prioritize information

- to read, think critically and draw conclusions from a given set of facts and opinions

- to "retool" and learn new ways of learning

Traditional academic subjects can provide a foundation for these abilities and for the development of adult intelligence *if they are taught so as to develop thinking and active curiosity about interesting ideas rather than rote-level memorization.* In this chapter, we'll tell you what you can do as parents to further this kind of independent thinking at home. So if the academic coaching we describe looks a bit different from the way you thought it would, celebrate with your child the chance to develop a well-tuned mind for the 21st century!

Support Your Child's Learning in Positive Ways

Parents as coaches play a powerful role in helping children develop good learning skills and attitudes for life-long success. Although you never signed up to be—nor should you be—a schoolteacher for your child, building a good relationship as collaborators in the learning process can be both productive and enjoyable for parent and child alike.

However, even the most skilled teachers and tutors often have trouble helping their own children with schoolwork. Because we care so much about how our children do in school, it's easy to fall into several dangerous traps. Instead of coaching, we may try to get overly involved, bossy or demanding. Often scenes or shouting matches result. We ourselves may not understand the work and feel uncomfortable admitting our "ignorance" in front of our child. We may try to "teach" something in a way different from the school's method, thus thoroughly confusing everybody. Sometimes the youngster decides it would be much more comfortable to avoid such situations all together and starts conveniently "forgetting" to bring work home.

Example

Mom: *"Any schoolwork to do at home tonight?"*

Child: *"Nah, I did it all at school."*

Mom: *"But your teacher said she wanted you to read with us at least 15 minutes every night."*

Child: *"Yeah, but every time we do, we just end up yelling at each other. I'd rather do it myself."*

Mom: *"Now listen here, young man. Reading is the most important thing you'll ever learn in school and you're not doing so hot, you know. You only got a "C" on your last report. You should be grateful you have parents who are willing to help you! Now get that book and sit down here."*

Child (sullen): *"The book's at school."*

Learning does not need to become a family battleground. Let's look at seven general principles for parental involvement that will make shared learning a challenge and a pleasure rather than a struggle.

Tips for Positive Coaching

1. Be available.
2. Offer support, not criticism.
3. Focus on effort and improvement instead of grades.
4. Remember, you don't have to be an expert.
5. Don't expect perfection.
6. Turn the thinking over to the child.
7. Enjoy!

Let's look at each one more closely.

1. Be Available

After a hard day of work, the last thing many of us feel like doing is expending more effort—reading to a four-year-old, going to the library or working on math facts with an elementary student or proofreading a teenager's science report. Nevertheless, your child needs to have you around, even if only for moral support. What's more, your child needs your attention as well as your physical presence. No matter how exciting a TV show is, you need to interrupt it if your child requests help in preparing for a quiz. While "grown-up" time for yourself is very important, try to arrange those much-needed breaks when your child is sleeping or otherwise engaged, and make yourself available during homework time.

2. Offer Support, Not Criticism

If you want your child to share his learning with you, follow some guidelines:

■ **Always find something positive to say before pointing out errors.** Let's say your seven-year-old shows you a story she has written:

> NO: *"That's a sort-of messy-looking paper, honey. Look here, for instance—you misspelled 'said' two times and we just finished studying that word for last week's test. I think you need to give it another try. You can do better than this."*

YES: *"What an interesting story! I like the original way you made the animals talk. And look at all the words you used to describe the dog. Would you like me to help you a little bit with some of the spelling words?"*
(Note: Check with your child's teacher to be sure any such corrections are within her guidelines. Many teachers want to see all mistakes themselves in order to know where more work is needed.)

Sometimes it is very hard to find something to praise about a child's piece of work. If it looks like something he dragged up from the swamp, try the following:

"You must have really tried hard to get started."

"This is a good start . . ."

"It looks as if you're trying to follow the directions."

"That certainly is a story (math paper, report, picture . . .)"

"Tell me a little bit about this assignment."

■ **Make your remarks honest and sincere.** Children have long antennae for false compliments, and research shows clearly that too much unearned praise actually reduces levels of motivation and self-esteem.

■ **Never attack the child personally.** Deal with the work at hand. Never be sarcastic, or you may expect your child to flee from further encounters.

Example

NO: *"How could you be so careless? Anyone can see that this is a minus sign and not a plus. How smart do you have to be to know the difference between adding and subtracting?"*

YES: *"I can see you worked hard, but it looks as if some of these problems were a little confusing for you. Why don't you go back and circle the plus or minus signs before you work out the answers. Then I'll be glad to look them over again."*

3. Focus on Effort and Improvement Instead of Grades

This rule is one of the most important for us to follow, but also one of the most difficult. Schools and parents have traditionally used grades as the main standard for judging children's progress, but current research shows clearly that:

1. while parents who have high expectations for their children produce better students, too much emphasis on grades alone lowers students' motivation to work.

2. to be a successful leader or even employee in a rapidly changing technological age, your child will need to feel that learning itself—not so much the grade he receives—is the important thing.

3. school grades are very bad predictors of how successful people will be in the real world.

While a certain emphasis on grades is necessary and inevitable for those who wish to attend competitive colleges, even some top colleges are now looking less at students' GPAs than at their interest and motivation to learn, their skill and involvement in non-academic areas (e.g., music, drama, community service, debate) and at their skills in working with other people. The best advice is to not ignore grades, but at the same time to place a stronger emphasis on the child's personal qualities, effort and improvement.

Examples

NO: *"What did you get on the test today? What did Stephen get?"*

"I don't care how hard you tried. You got a C- !"

"Let me get this straight. You got a B instead of an A because you got interested in working out one of the longer problems and spent too much time on it? How do you ever expect to get into college?"

YES: *"I know you're not satisfied with your grade on that test. Let's talk about what you can do to study more effectively."*

"I'm so pleased to see you taking a real interest in the topic you're studying in history class. It's important to think about those issues and not just memorize the information for the test."

"We need to talk about your report card. I'm disappointed that your teachers say you're causing a disturbance in class. I know you're still getting good grades, but we also care a lot about how good a citizen you are at school."

4. Remember, You Don't Have to Be an Expert

It is the school's job to teach your child. If you find yourself constantly having to introduce or explain new learning, it's time for a conference at school. Nevertheless, there will undoubtedly be times when you must work with concepts or skills with which you are unfamiliar. The most important rule here is: *Don't be afraid to say, "I don't know."* It's a big mistake to blunder along pretending you understand something and probably confusing your child even further.

Don't be afraid to say, "I don't know."

Many of us are somewhat boggled by today's new and different ways of presenting math concepts, for example. In such cases, your job is to show your child that you, too, are still a learner and don't know everything already. Perhaps you could find a reference source or a page in the textbook that would help you learn more about the topic with your child. If both you and your child are confused, however, you should probably turn the responsibility back to the student and the teacher.

Example

"I'm sorry, honey, but I just can't help you anymore with this problem. I never had problems like this in school—they taught so differently back then. You'll need to get help from your teacher. First thing in the morning, why don't you make an appointment to meet with him? You know, you're lucky you're learning to use math to solve real-life problems."

If you are embarrassed about the level of your own skills—in reading, for example—you might as well "fess up" to your child. Here is a golden opportunity to demonstrate the importance of learning to you.

Example

NO: *"You want me to read with you? Ah . . . well, not right now. I'm really very busy. Go read by yourself and then you can tell me about it."*

YES: *"I'm so glad you want me to read with you, but one of the things I've regretted most about my own school years is that I never got to be as good a reader as I wished. I'll be glad to read with you, but you must understand that I'm still trying hard myself to become a better reader. Maybe we can help each other—I don't want you to go through life being embarrassed about reading as I have. Remember, your teacher said it would be okay to listen to that book on tape, too. I'd enjoy that."*

Note: Books on tape are available at most libraries, and some teachers encourage their use as a back-up (not a substitute) for reading. Make sure your child's teacher approves, however, before suggesting this alternative.

5. Don't Expect Perfection

A fourth-grade teacher I once knew lost patience one day with her class. "How can you act so childish?" she demanded. As the children looked innocently up at her, she confessed she had to laugh at herself.

Children need to know that you care about their achievements, but remember that they are, after all, just kids. Setting your standards too high is a sure prescription for either a sullen, turned-off youngster or for one who is so nervous, anxious and perfectionistic that she makes her life—and everyone else's—miserable. Research shows that good students tend to come from homes free from unrealistic restrictions or pressures.

It is also a mistake to expect equally expert performance in every subject or skill. Many outstanding mathematicians are terrible spellers, and some excellent readers have difficulty in gym class. Since your child probably inherited some of his talents (and liabilities) from you, try to be understanding and help him set realistic goals for improvement, not perfection.

6. Turn the Thinking Over to the Child

A common parental trap is to end up doing the work for the child, which is often easier than struggling through to help her understand it herself. You can avoid this pitfall if you keep asking yourself the question, "Whose job/responsibility/problem is this?" Consider some scenarios:

- A parent of a four-year-old asks him to pick up his blocks. Child ignores parent and wanders off to another activity. Parent picks up the blocks.

- Dad is helping seven-year-old Susie with a math problem that she does not understand. Finally, in frustration, he tells her the answer.

- A nine-year-old has procrastinated on a science fair project. Grandma buys the supplies and completes the project.

■ A 12-year-old has a book report due tomorrow. Mother stays up until midnight to edit and type it.

In each of these cases, the parent has stolen from the child the opportunity to learn—not only academic skills, but also responsibility and the natural consequences of behavior. These habits are far more important in the long run than completing a single assignment or getting the situation superficially resolved. Please do not be so eager to "save" your child temporary discomfort that you rob her of a chance to learn these important skills for life! If an assignment is not done, the child will (and should) suffer the consequences at school. If work is not understood or is too difficult, camouflaging the child's difficulty deprives child and teacher of the opportunity to straighten out the confusion.

Please do not be so eager to "save" your child temporary discomfort that you rob her of a chance to learn important skills for life!

Many teachers give assignments to learn what the child understands, not to get back a perfect paper. I have worked with several children who ended up in serious academic difficulty because they never received the help they needed at school. Since their work was always well done (by the parents), the teachers never realized the depth of their problems.

One of the most important things you can give your children is the ability to take responsibility for their own thinking and behavior. Homes for good learners emphasize independent problem solving from the beginning. Preschoolers are encouraged to complete tasks by themselves, such as tie their shoes and set the table; older children are expected to think through problems.

Homes for good learners emphasize independent problem solving from the beginning.

7. Enjoy!

Our brains learn best when we are excited about what we are learning, when we feel safe and secure and when some enjoyment, humor or novelty is part of the experience. Even routine drill assignments, such

as memorizing the multiplication tables, will stick better if some fun is attached (for example, you can make up silly stories, songs or drawings for number combinations). The more fun you and your child can have learning together, the better the lifetime habits that you are teaching. This teaching job is perhaps a parent's most important one: Learning is fun, interesting and worth the effort it takes. If you convey these attitudes to your children, you are equipping them for success in life far beyond the school doors.

Learning is fun, interesting and worth the effort it takes.

The Learning Journey: Coaching from Preschool to High School

Our parental involvement in the learning process changes as children grow older. A wise observer once remarked that the purpose of parenthood should be "planned obsolescence"; that is, we gradually phase ourselves out of taking responsibility for our children as we encourage them to fulfill their own lives and personalities. If we help them lay the right foundations, we can confidently send them forth to grapple with the new challenges of a new century.

The Young Child

Parents of children up to age seven have the most responsibility—and maybe the most fun, too! Their primary concern with learning should

It is not the job of parents to drill young children on alphabets or math facts, but rather to develop the mental structures that will enable them to understand these symbolic forms of learning when the right time comes.

be to build a wide, rich foundation of experience, language and problem-solving skills for further learning. It is not the job of parents to drill young children on alphabets or math facts, but rather to develop the mental structures that will enable them to understand these symbolic forms of learning when the right time comes. How do we build these mental structures? By providing something like a cafeteria of experience, with lots of interesting, enticing and challenging projects and activities to engage the child's curiosity. Early childhood experience should leave children with the *attitudes* they'll need for *school success:*

■ I like learning.

■ I am good at doing new things.

■ If something seems hard at first, I can get it by trying.

■ Grown-ups will help me if I need it, but they don't butt in when I am trying to learn something on my own.

■ It is fun to play with other kids. I know how to cooperate with them.

■ I can't have my own way all the time. Sometimes I must listen to grown-ups and do as they say.

■ I like to be helpful.

Parents who help young children internalize these feelings will have a much easier job later when it comes time to reinforce school learning. (See Chapter 5 for more about how to help build these important attitudes.)

The Elementary Child

As children move through the elementary grades, their parents' roles should mainly be those of coach, cheering section and planning assistant. The guidelines in this chapter should help you be an effective coach, but it's also important to keep up that cheering section that says to your child, "We believe in you, and we're here to help when you need us." During this period, most children also need a little assistance with the logistics of daily school life: organizing school supplies, planning long-term assignments, arranging transportation to libraries and reference sources. Gradually, as the youngster gains maturity and experience, he can take over more and more responsibility for himself.

The Teen

If good foundations have been laid, parents of adolescents can pull more of their support back to the sidelines. Teenagers, especially middle schoolers, still need strong cheering sections and the under-

standing that help is available if needed, but they are naturally impelled to try to muddle through themselves whenever possible. Parents of teen-aged students should not have to organize their youngsters' assignments or become "tutors" at home. If your child is overwhelmed and floundering, consult with the school immediately about obtaining special help.

Parents of teens can help by keeping up with topics covered in school. For example, your youngster may be willing to discuss some of the issues she's hearing about in a social studies course, or themes from a book she's reading in English class. She'll enjoy the conversation more if you're tuned in to what she's been studying. Most importantly, she may need a sounding board for the confusing array of new ideas available to her developing adolescent brain. (See *Your Child's Growing Mind,* by Jane M. Healy, Ph.D., Doubleday, Inc., 1994, for more information on this fascinating—and sometimes exasperating—age group.) If your youngster feels comfortable asking you for help, it's okay to offer practical assistance in such areas as proofreading assignments, memorizing for quizzes or thinking up ideas for projects.

If you follow these general guidelines, you'll establish an environment in which you can be an effective coach while still respecting your child's changing needs. In the next two chapters we will look at your role in reinforcing specific forms of learning: reading, writing and spelling, math and science.

Chapter 7

COACHING YOUR CHILD IN READING

What Is Good Reading?

Most parents realize that reading is a fundamental academic skill, but not everyone is aware of exactly what "good reading" is all about. Many of us were taught that reading is mainly sounding out words, and that the way to make a child into a good reader is to drill on "phonics." Of course, the sound patterns and sequences of sounds in words are critical to reading success, but now we know that language and thinking skills are equally important.

Children who learn to sound out words without understanding what they mean end up with reading comprehension problems that may restrict their progress all through school. Good reading comprehension starts with:

- the ability to understand spoken language.

- the ability to remember and think about ideas.

- the understanding that the reader's job is to get the writer's message.

- an active mental effort to understand what is read.

- the ability to make connections between new ideas and previous learning.

- interesting reading material.

- curiosity.

Many schools now place more emphasis on "real" books (good novels, nonfiction books) than on reading textbooks ("basals"), and encourage students to read for information and pleasure as well as for drill. However your child's school approaches reading, you can help by emphasizing the meaning of what is read and helping your child to understand the story and ideas presented. While such devices as flash cards can still sometimes be useful for learning word accuracy, it is important to concentrate on words in meaningful sentences whenever possible.

Don't try to force ("teach") your child to read before he is ready. When he starts asking questions about words ("What does 'm-i-l-k' spell?" "What does that word say?"), answer them, but don't make an issue of it. You don't want to create a reading problem. Instead, follow these guidelines for laying a solid groundwork. They are even more important than learning the A-B-Cs!

Building a Strong Reading Foundation

1. Read aloud to your children, or listen together to tapes of good books.

Try to establish a regular time for reading aloud. If you are shaky about your reading ability, you may need to let a good tape

The amount of time your child spends listening to someone read aloud will be the best predictor of reading scores.

do the job. Try to get tapes with associated books, so you and your child can listen and follow along at the same time. Many school libraries have these coordinated sets of books and tapes. Discuss what is being read: **predict** ("What will happen next?"); **encourage analysis** ("Why do you think she made that decision; was it a good one?"); **reinforce memory** ("Let's remind ourselves of the order of events that happened in the chapter we read yesterday."). The amount of time your child spends listening to someone read aloud will be the best predictor of reading scores. Do not stop reading aloud when the child learns to read: Elementary and middle school children still need this important experience.

2. Encourage language development by talking and listening to each other.

Television does not do the trick, as the language is too often "dumbed down"; moreover, viewers tend to pay attention to what they see rather than what they hear. Limit and regulate TV time and *make a point to talk together as a family*—at meals, in the car, during family activities, whenever possible—without the distraction of "the tube." Give children access to a wide range of experiences and discuss and relive them together. (*How to Have Intelligent and Creative Conversations with Your Kids,* by Jane M. Healy, Ph.D., Doubleday, Inc. 1994, offers abundant suggestions for mind-stretching family discussions.)

3. Help your children to be analytic thinkers.

Children need quiet time to mull over ideas, and they need encouragement in expressing them. Most kids are capable of far more complex thinking than we give them credit for. Don't hesitate to ask your children's well-considered opinions about all manner of things in your daily life: TV shows, current events, people's attitudes, school activities, family decisions. Ask for reasons why they think as they do. Listen as they express their ideas and state your own without putting theirs down. If you expand rather than correct their conversation and let them participate in decision-making, they will feel important and believe their ideas have value.

4. Show your children that reading can be fun.

Your own use and enjoyment of books, magazines and newspapers is also a good predictor of your children's reading success. What better way to show your children that reading is a pleasure—not a forced march through difficult or boring lessons—than to enjoy it yourself. Even if you've never been an enthusiastic (or very good) reader, you can still try to spend some time with printed material. You may also want to confide in your children if you believe that better reading skills would have made life more interesting for you.

Fundamental Language Skills

Reading (and also writing or speaking) requires mastery of four fundamental language skills: **phonology, syntax, semantics** and **pragmatics.** Helping your child develop them gives her a boost toward doing well in all subjects (and in life!).

Phonology: sorting out the *sounds* in words and putting them in order.

1. **Make sure your youngster has lots of opportunities to listen to people talk clearly, face-to-face.** Television talk is usually too quick and garbled for clear reception by the child's brain.

2. **Play oral word games, particularly those involving rhymes or letter reversals (such as pig latin).** Go to the library and ask for a book of language games.

3. **Expect your child to listen.** If he seems to have difficulty, ask him to repeat what he thinks you said.

4. **Give clear directions and expect your child to follow them.** Start with one or two ("Please get a bar of soap and bring it to the kitchen"), and work up to longer series.

5. **If your child appears to have repeated difficulty speaking clearly (articulation), hearing different sounds in words or remembering what she hears, seek an evaluation from the school's speech/language therapist or a clinic.**

Syntax: understanding how words go together in order to make meaningful sentences ("syntax" is a fancy word for grammar).

1. **Choose books to read aloud to your child that contain good language.** Stop and focus on individual sentences; talk about how the words go together to convey an idea. ("I like the way this author used such colorful words to describe the pony." "Let's see, it says they launched the boat; who are 'they' in this sentence?")

2. **Find opportunities to expose your children to language that is more "book-like" than that which they hear in the everyday world.** (Ask your librarian for read-aloud suggestions or tapes of high quality stories, the latter especially if you are self-conscious about your own use of grammar.)

3. **Listen to your child's language.** If you hear grammatical errors in his speech at any age ("He wented to the movies"), gently model a better form ("Yes, he went to the movies"). Persistence of such errors long after other children of the same age have mastered these rules is a signal to seek a professional evaluation.

4. **Show your child how to use more complicated sentences.** ("He went to the movies because he thought the show looked exciting.")

5. **Don't worry about trying to teach the names of parts of speech (nouns, verbs, adjectives) to young children.** They learn them from hearing good examples.

Semantics: understanding the meaning of individual words, sentences or text (closely related to reading comprehension).

1. **Be on the alert for opportunities to help your child add to his vocabulary.** For example, if you are reading a story together, pick out interesting or difficult words, check the meanings, then practice using them.

2. **Try learning a "word of the week" with the whole family.** Each week, choose a new word and write it on a card, along with examples of sentences in which it is used correctly. Challenge yourselves to find examples in print and use the word frequently in conversation during the week.

3. **When reading with young children, ask questions using the "five w's": who, what, when, where, why . . . and how.** For older children, ask them to summarize what the story is about. Together, develop some questions you would like to ask the author. Try to answer them.

4. **Encourage your child to express opinions about stories or articles.** You don't always have to agree with the author. For older students, try comparing two articles on the same topic. Do the authors have similar points of view? How well do they make their points?

5. **Practice making "mental movies" to encourage accurate understanding and memory of what is read.** ("Let's close our eyes and imagine what the monster in the story looks like. What color is your monster? Tell me more about his appearance.") Read some books without pictures, or read the story aloud before showing the pictures. Discuss together the pictures that came into your minds during reading.

6. **Encourage your child to engage in hobbies, collections, projects, games and spontaneous play.** Even such simple activities as pouring sand or driving nails into a birdhouse build reasoning skills necessary for understanding. For older children, family trips or shared chores (washing the car, weeding the garden) offer good opportunities for talking and thinking together.

Pragmatics: knowing how or why people use words socially; understanding where others are "coming from."

1. **Start talking and listening to your child early in her life.** Even if you have neglected this opportunity, it's never too late!

2. **Teach your child how to use language politely.** ("Please," "thank you," "excuse me, but . . . ," etc.) Do not accept rude language.

3. **Encourage your child to play with other children.** Do not let him spend all his time with video or computer games, but make sure he learns to play, imagine and negotiate rules with groups of his peers.

4. **Talk about why people say what they do.** ("Why do you think the salesman told us that the toy was so sturdy when it wasn't? Maybe he was anxious to get our money!") Help your child realize that not everyone thinks as she does and that her playmates have their own motivations. ("I know you want to play with Johnny, but I'm not surprised he doesn't want to go out. He's probably upset because his dog is sick.") A child who can understand others' points of view is much better equipped to understand where an author is "coming from"—one of the cornerstones of reading comprehension.

In fact, although many of these skills may seem far removed from sounding out words on a page, research shows that each part of the language/thinking equation has its own special relationship to reading success!

Good Language + Good Thinking = Good Reading

Different Help for Different Ages

As children grow in the reading process, your role will change. Let's look at how you can use your time most constructively.

Helping the Young Child and Beginning Reader

1. **Keep the level of pressure low.** Some children learn to read by themselves at age four, and some won't learn until they are about eight. Generally, this development has little to do with intelligence, and many late readers soon catch up. If you are laying a good groundwork by following the previous suggestions, don't get impatient and try to force reading on your child! Parents who do usually regret it because they get a turned-off youngster and sometimes even the start of an unnecessary "learning disability." If you have serious concerns about late reading, seek the help of a qualified reading specialist or school psychologist.

2. **Recognize your child's anxiety.** Reassure your child that, while reading is important, he will learn when he is ready. Keep it fun and interesting.

3. **Flash cards are not the best way to teach your child about reading.** We now know that children learn words better when they see them in context; that is, in a sentence that has personal meaning to them. Moreover, I have known children who developed a lifelong aversion to print after being subjected to early flash-card drills. Read to him instead.

4. **It is fine to teach your child the alphabet and to point out different letters on signs—as long as you don't force the issue.**

When your child starts to ask questions about printed words, answer them.

5. **Don't panic if your child reverses letters or words ("tab" for "bat").** These confusions are natural for young children and usually sort themselves out around age eight.

6. **If your child has any sign of language difficulty in the four fundamental language skills listed earlier, was late to talk, mixes up words or can't pronounce words appropriately, get a thorough evaluation from your school's speech/language therapist or a clinic.** This is especially important if anyone in your family has had a reading problem.

7. **If your home is bilingual, you should probably concentrate on one language for beginning reading experiences, although you may wish to continue to read to your child in both languages.** If the child seems confused, however, try to limit all reading experiences to one language as much as possible until the confusion passes.

8. **Use picture books.** Take turns with your child telling a story from the pictures.

9. **Practice naming words that start with the same consonant sound—mug, mother, missile, mess.**

10. **Play rhyming games, read children's poems and call attention to rhyming sounds.**

Helping Elementary Students

To help the teacher develop your child's reading ability, continue daily story time, express interest and enthusiasm about school progress and let the child read to you at home every day. Your job is not to teach, but to reinforce good reading habits. Here are some guidelines:

1. **Set aside a regular time to read to your child.** As she learns to read, add ten minutes a day when she can read to you. Continue regularly until silent reading ability is gradually established.

2. **Make sure that the child is reading from books that are easy and enjoyable.** This is called the "independent" level of reading. If you have any questions, ask the teacher. The purpose is not to teach skills but to practice fluency and learn to enjoy reading.

3. **Let the child choose the books, as long as they are at the independent level.** Children sometimes try to please their parents by selecting "hard" books, but this is a self-defeating exercise.

4. **As the child reads, listen to determine if she understands the meaning.** Clues are found in the way she phrases, observes punctuation marks or makes comments about the story.

5. **Insert an occasional question that will challenge her thinking and to which there is *no one right answer*.** "Why do you think John wanted those shoes?" "What do you think will happen next?" "Let's guess

what they could find in the old barn." "What might have happened if he had stayed home from the picnic?" Don't focus on literal-level questions like, "What color were the shoes?" "What did they take on the picnic?"

6. **The most common error adults (including teachers) make is helping too much.** If the child mispronounces a word, remain silent. Listen to the rest of the phrase or sentence to see if the mispronunciation changed the meaning. For example, if the phrase "a little dog" is read "a little doggy," I recommend you leave it alone. For beginning readers, confusion of "a" and "the" may also be ignored. If the child makes errors that change the sense of the story, wait for her to realize that meaning has been lost. You want her to monitor the meaning herself. If she continues, stop her at the end of a sentence or paragraph. Ask, "Did that make sense?" Encourage her to listen and reread for meaning. If a word is too difficult, have her read to the end of the sentence and try to figure out the missing word. If not, supply it.

7. **Remember, perfection is not the goal.** Comprehension is.

8. **When the story is finished, ask her to retell it** *briefly***.** Help her find only the main ideas and important parts and recall them in order. This process of synthesis is difficult but important. Encourage quality rather than quantity in retelling.

9. **If you are both interested, extend your discussion of the story.** You could imagine another ending, a different main character or a different setting. Children enjoy creative projects: acting out scenes, making models of the setting in a shoebox or even rewriting the plot from another point of view. Such projects can be taken to school and shared with the class. They are far more interesting than the standard book report!

10. **You can help your child with one of comprehension's greatest tools if you encourage mental imagery.** Practice making "mental movies" of what is happening in the book. Try drawing pictures of what you each "saw" in the story. Use books without pictures or cover them up so that you can get your own ideas. Research shows that good comprehenders instinctively make mental pictures when they read, and that poorer readers' comprehension can be improved by direct instruction in this important strategy.

11. **If your child resists reading to you at home, reflect on the amount of pressure in the situation.** Are the sessions too long? Should you get easier books? Are you expecting perfection? Are you giving enough praise? Do you take a turn reading now and then? If a real problem seems to exist, go to the teacher or the reading specialist with your questions.

12. **Encourage habits of independent reading.** Extending bedtime is still a good inducement. Turn off the TV and let the whole family read together. Despite all our efforts, children learn to read by reading.

(Material in "Helping Elementary Students" from *Your Child's Growing Mind*, by Jane M. Healy, Ph.D., Doubleday, Inc. 1994.)

Reading with Your Teen

By this time, your role should have diminished to one of support and occasional coaching. Do not stop reading aloud as a family, and let the youngster help choose the books or topics of interest. Sample a wide variety: novels with important themes, poetry, essays, newspaper editorials, plays, humor. Set aside sufficient time for discussion. Listen to your teen's ideas without criticizing or asserting your opinion. Young people at this age need to experiment with lots of different ways of looking at the world, and sometimes their "off-the-wall" ideas are *necessary steps to adult thinking.*

Listen to your teen's ideas without criticizing or asserting your opinion.

Whether they admit it or not, many teenagers still enjoy family times for word games or games that build grammar skills ("Mad Libs") or vocabulary ("Scrabble," "Pictionary"). Don't underrate the importance of your availability and modeling of interest in such activities. In one family, the teenage daughter seemed to believe she was far too sophisticated for such things until she saw her mom and a friend enjoying weekly games of "Scrabble." Pretty soon the young lady was hovering nearby—and before long became a regular part of the game.

You are not expected to have the expertise to help your teen with specific study skills; this job should be covered by the school. One particularly useful strategy sometimes gets overlooked by teachers, however, and you may find it helpful.

SQ3R

One nifty technique that is helpful with textbook reading for students nine and older is called SQ3R, which stands for:

1. Survey
2. Question
3. Read
4. Recite
5. Review

If your child's teacher has not introduced SQ3R, you can show your child how to use it for history, science, literature or other texts. Here's how:

1. **Survey:** Look over the entire assignment or chapter. Read the title. Read all the subheadings. Look at any maps, charts, pictures. How do they all fit together? Skim the first and the last paragraphs. Survey study guides at the end of the chapter. How does this chapter relate to the entire book? To the course? Assure your child that the time spent on this step is not wasted, but will cut down on total study time.

2. **Question:** Who wrote this and why? Why am I reading it (for fun, for a test, to learn about how to make widgets)? What will it be about? Think of some questions inspired by the title (e.g., *Building the Colonies*: What were the colonies? Where were they? What did the colonists need to build? Homes? Stores? Factories? Governments? How did they build them? Who did the work?). Try to guess how to answer the questions. This step gets the child personally involved, setting his own direction and reasons for reading. Turn all the chapter topic headings into questions. Try to guess answers to these and to any questions given in the text.

3. **Read:** Now read the chapter carefully. Writing summaries of each section in the margin is a good habit to acquire. Most students tend to underline too much. Read first, then go back and highlight only the most important points.

4. **Recite:** Without looking back at the text, try to answer the questions you asked at the beginning. How do all these subtopics fit together? What are the main ideas in this chapter? What are the important facts and details? How are the pictures, charts and maps related to the topic?

5. **Review:** Go back over the material after some time has passed. Refresh your memory of the important facts and ideas. Periodic review is the best way to create memory circuits. Make study guides of facts and ideas that must be remembered.

SQ3R is only one of many practical tools to help students' reading comprehension. Many good teachers now ask students to list ideas, discuss or write about a topic before starting to read about it, and are finding interesting and motivating ways to combine reading, writing and reasoning in every subject. Check to see if your school is working on this integration of skills. Encourage teachers to keep up with new research that helps children read with their brains instead of only with their eyes and voices.

(Material in "SQ3R" from *Your Child's Growing Mind*, by Jane M. Healy, Ph.D., Doubleday, Inc. 1994.)

Troubleshooting

How do you know when to be worried? Danger signals differ depending on the age of the child.

Early Signs

■ Repeated ear infections; hearing impairment or loss.

■ Language delay or problems at any age. Most reading problems are related to language disability.

■ Persistent problems with paying attention.

■ Uncorrected vision problems. Be sure to have your child checked early for amblyopia (lazy eye).

■ Family history of language, reading, spelling or writing problems.

■ Left-handedness or ambidexterity, *if* there are other signals. (Many left-handers are fine readers.)

■ Protracted difficulty telling time, learning telephone numbers or addresses, tying shoes, following directions. All require sequencing, handled in the area of the brain that also puts words and sounds in order.

■ Difficulty processing material quickly through eyes or ears. Current research indicates dyslexia may result from brain-based differences in interpreting rapidly changing signals in both the visual and auditory realms.

During School Years

- Reversals or confusion of letters, words, numerals, directions or ideas that persist after age seven or eight and are accompanied by other symptoms. All young children reverse letters. It does not mean they will be dyslexic. Please don't make an issue of this with your child!! Tension can make normal developmental errors into real problems.

- Unhappiness in school; physical symptoms (stomachaches, nightmares, worries) that can't be otherwise explained.

- Eye problems or headaches. Although most reading problems are in the brain, eye problems may also contribute.

- Schoolwork brought home that is consistently too difficult for the child to do.

- Labored oral reading and difficulty with comprehension on material that the school sends home.

- Difficulty getting the meaning while reading silently after age eight.

- Problems with writing, spelling or foreign languages. Bright children may be dyslexic without showing severe reading difficulty. Their problems with language symbols show up when they have to write them down or master a new system.

A parent's main job is to stay attuned to the school's ability to meet a child's special needs. If you find yourself forced to teach reading, rather than just reinforcing it at home, something is wrong. The parent-child relationship is too precious to clutter up with pressures from inappropriate school demands. If trouble is brewing in your house, go to the school and try to get at the source of the difficulty.

(Material in "Troubleshooting" from *Your Child's Growing Mind,* by Jane M. Healy, Ph.D., Doubleday, Inc. 1994.)

Reading experiences with your child can be a wonderful window into his development and provide mutual enjoyment and a starting point for interesting conversations. No matter how good (or poor) a reader you are, you can share in your child's process of learning to use the valuable tool of reading for a lifetime of mental stimulation and enjoyment.

Dyslexia

Somewhere between 10 and 20 percent of the population, often people of average or above-average intelligence, show some symptoms of Specific Reading Disability (sometimes called "Specific Language Disability" or "Dyslexia"). This difficulty is not a reflection of basic intelligence! It is often present in highly creative families and is thought to be inherited. It may show up in several ways:

■ confusion of sounds in speech and/or other language delay

■ delayed mastery of early reading skills

■ poor spelling

■ difficulty getting ideas down on paper in an organized way

■ slow reading

■ poor oral reading

■ difficulty learning foreign languages

Unfortunately, some school psychologists have not been sufficiently alerted to this problem, so youngsters, especially bright ones, may slip through the diagnostic cracks. If you suspect your child may be in this category, consult the Recommended Reading list for further reading and resources. A child with a learning difference needs good professional help to avoid becoming an alienated, "unmotivated" or depressed youngster.

Helping with Writing and Spelling

Current Educational Views

With the advent of the computer, attitudes about the basic skills of spelling and writing are changing. While it is still of primary importance to be able to express ideas clearly—on paper or in conversation—computers are helping many students refine the "mechanics" of the writing process, particularly handwriting and spelling. Schools are placing more emphasis and time on the thought process and less time on teaching these specific skills. This change in attitudes is hard for many parents to understand, but it makes sense if you want your child to gain the advanced skills necessary for getting and keeping her job in the 21st century. We must not give up the so-called "basics," but we must also be practical about the most appropriate uses of computer and human brains.

Take spelling, for example. The fact is that some people have a real predisposition to be good spellers, and vice versa—and it's not in the least way related to intelligence! Doubtless this discrepancy results from inherited abilities in auditory processing (the brain's ability to grasp the sounds in words, tell them apart and put them in order) and visual memory for little strings of written symbols (words). It is still important for schools to teach the basic rules of spelling (why do you double the "n" at the end of "run" when adding "ing"?). For those who simply can't seem to learn to spell despite good teaching, however, the computer with a spell-checker has been a lifesaver. Probably the best idea is to give your child a solid learning background and some help with mechanics (see below), expect the school to teach spelling well and—if it simply doesn't work—let the student use a spell-checker and go on to more important things. Many very intelligent people have grown up with an "I'm dumb" complex simply because they weren't by nature talented spellers. Never imply that a child is "dumb" if she has difficulty with spelling!

Nevertheless, life experiences and teaching can make a big difference in spelling ability. Many teachers are distressed about the low level of auditory skills in the TV generation, and with good reason: Too much watching of TV and playing with video games can deprive those brain circuits connected to careful, analytical listening—and spelling. As in reading, one of the best foundations for good spelling you can give your child is to build up brain circuits for good, careful listening—without any pictures attached! Unfortunately, the visual input from TV doesn't help when it comes to building visual memory for words. Having your child follow along while you read aloud or reading independently is the secret here.

Too much watching of TV and playing with video games can deprive those brain circuits connected to careful, analytical listening—and spelling.

Likewise, the handwriting of today's students has suffered from lack of emphasis and practice. Before we march angrily on the schools, however, we need to remember that there is a great deal to teach in a rapidly changing technological age. Schools these days realize that, first and foremost, they must spend their precious hours teaching kids to think, to analyze, to respond intelligently to change and to express themselves in a forceful and organized manner for the "communication age." Consequently, they may very well have to cut down on drill time (some call it "drill-and-kill!"). Learning the rules of punctuation and sentence structure should still be viewed as important, however.

Many schools today are taking the sensible middle ground: Teach and practice handwriting in grades 1-4, but don't make it a great issue if a child then needs help from a computer keyboard. When your children are adults, they will probably do little handwriting; in fact, even by the time today's primary students are in high school, they will likely be taking class notes on a laptop computer provided by the school.

What really counts in a communication age are such skills as planning how to get thoughts down in an appropriate order, using good sentences that express these thoughts and developing an argument (a thesis) in a logical manner. So here we are back to the same basic language and thinking foundations that we saw in reading. Good writers are usually those who have absorbed the sound of language from books—both from listening and reading.

Good writers are usually those who have absorbed the sound of language from books—both from listening and reading.

How to Help with the Mechanics of Writing and Spelling

Helping the Young Child

1. **Make sure your child has plenty of finger and thumb exercises to build muscles for handwriting.** Handcrafts, cooking and cutting activities, hobbies and needlework all build fine muscle coordination and strength.

2. **Don't force pencils on young children until they are ready to hold them properly.** Once faulty pencil grip is established, it is almost impossible to correct. Show your child how to grip the pencil between the end of the thumb and first finger of the writing hand, with the middle finger underneath, supporting the pencil. If the child can't control the pencil with the ends of his fingers and has to shove it into the center of his hand, he is not ready to use it. Stick to paintbrushes and easels or chalk on a chalkboard until the circuits are more mature.

3. **Help your child make his own books.** Provide scrap paper, crayons, pencils (if he's ready), markers, staplers, paste, old magazines to cut up and wallpaper samples (free from stores) for covers. You can be the "secretary" and write captions, comments or stories for the child, following his dictation. Covering pages with transparent "contact"-type paper makes the book seem very important.

4. **Let your child see you writing (shopping lists, letters, notes) and explain how useful writing is in your life.** Help her prepare a letter to Grandma or a friend.

5. **Follow the suggestions in Chapter 7 about building phonological (speech sounds) skills.** Help your child make a picture book of magazine cut-outs that illustrate the first sounds of alphabet letters. Try to focus on sounds, not the  way the word is spelled visually. For example, "ship" looks as if it starts with "s," but the first sound is really "sh"; "cake" starts with a "c," but the sound is that of "k."

6. **Once your child can hear first sounds, work with final sounds.** (What's the last sound in "ran," "box," "paintbrush"?) Read lots of rhymes and listen for the rhyming words, then make some up. As children get older, they may be able to listen for the number of syllables in the word. Practice clapping once for each syllable ("bi-cy-cle," "ad-ver-tise-ment"). If no one ever taught you this, you may improve your own listening and spelling skills in the bargain!

7. **Good spellers notice the details of words.** They can easily tell letters apart ("visual discrimination") and remember them. Help your child develop visual discrimination skills by looking carefully for details in pictures. Encourage children to be careful observers of the environment—shapes of leaves, flowers, work materials. "Hidden pictures" or visual search games/books are useful here.

8. **Inquire about the school's policy regarding beginning spelling.** Some schools encourage children to use "Invented Spelling"; emphasis is placed on the child hearing the sounds in a word and writing what he thinks it sounds like rather than memorizing the perfect form. Follow the school's guidelines on this issue and praise your child's efforts without finding fault. If your child is not making the transition into standard (correct) spelling by the end of second grade, consider it a possible danger sign signaling a need for some special help.

Helping Elementary Students and Teens

Note: Please modify these suggestions according to your confidence in your own writing and spelling skills. If you are concerned that you don't know it all, please believe that this does not make you a "bad parent," nor will it doom your child to failure. Do your best, and depend on the teacher to be the final judge. One mother who was embarrassed about her writing skills and lack of a high school diploma decided to sign up for a noncredit writing course at her local community college. To her amazement, she was a good adult student; eventually she passed the GED and several years later became the proud recipient of an associate degree. Meanwhile her kids cheered her on, and "homework" time took on a new meaning every evening as the family hit the books! It's never too late to show our children that learning is an important, life-long pursuit—-and to grow a few new brain cells yourself!

1. **If you are reasonably comfortable with the task, and the teacher approves, be available (be *unavoidable*, if necessary) to help proofread papers.** Remember to start with positive comments. If you find an error, make a mark in the margin ("s" for spelling, "p" for punctuation, "g" for a grammatical error); sit down with your child and see if he can detect the error. Use a dictionary together to check uncertain spellings. If these sessions turn into shouting matches, back off and reread Chapters 4 and 6.

2. **Help your child learn to spell better by practicing with groups of "word families"—words that all contain the same part, such as "sing, string, thing, bringing"; "catch, match, scratch."**

3. **Use a "multisensory" approach to reinforce spelling words:** Look at the word, talk about the letter patterns it contains ("Va-ca-tion. Look, I see two-letter syllables ending with 'a' and 'tion' at the end.") and relate it to known rules or patterns. Eventually, ask your child to tell you about the patterns in the word. Have the child say the word aloud while writing it, then cover it up and say and write it again and then once again. Some children like to practice writing with an index finger on a rough surface, such as the living room rug. Be sure they say the word aloud as they are writing. Writing words or syllables in different colors also helps some youngsters. The old practice of writing a word 20 times in a column is not a very good technique, as it is boring, doesn't engage the higher thinking centers and too often leads to practicing wrong spellings.

4. **Discuss the reasons for rules *if you are familiar with them*.** Why do we capitalize proper names? Why should items in a series be separated by commas? Why do we put different kinds of punctuation at the end of sentences? Point out punctuation

elements when you are reading together and discuss why they make the writing more interesting or understandable.

5. **Encourage your child to read pieces of writing aloud and try to catch her own errors.** Encourage her to do a "first draft" to get the ideas down, and then go back and tidy up the mechanics.

Helping Your Child to Be a Better Writer

You may realize by now that being a good "technician" is not enough to make a child a good writer. I have received plenty of papers (even from graduate students) that were spelled and punctuated correctly— but had nothing to say! In the long run, content—the quality, clarity and organization of ideas—is what matters, although decent presentation is necessary to make the good ideas understandable. Here are a few tips to help youngsters of all ages improve content and organization:

1. **Encourage your child to keep a journal to get in the habit of daily writing.** This practice can be especially important in the summer, when you want to keep skills alive. The actual product is much less important here than the process—the habit of getting ideas down easily and regularly. Try keeping a journal yourself and devoting a special time of day to journal writing with your child. Decide whether you wish to read these aloud to each other. This activity is especially good on family trips.

2. **Make reference books (dictionary, encyclopedia, dictionary of quotations) available or know where they are kept in the public library.** A paperback thesaurus (synonym dictionary) is useful for "dressing up" a composition by substituting more interesting words. There are versions even for young children.

3. **Practice family storytelling.** Tell round-robin stories in which

each participant adds a brief episode before passing to a new narrator. Many of us are embarrassed and feel a little awkward when attempting storytelling for the first time. Try something familiar, such as an account of an event from your own school days. Children also love adventure stories with themselves as the main character:

Examples

"One day Jeff went out in the woods to play and he discovered a big box of gold under an oak tree."

Or go off-the-wall:
"Once upon a time there was this six-headed monster, a purple six-headed monster. He lived in a cave. One day he went out for something to eat and he found . . . ."

Have the next storyteller finish the sentence and start another piece of the story. Let it get as fanciful as you like, and don't be afraid to laugh and be a little silly. You'll get better as you practice—and you'll have some fun in the bargain.

4. When the child is trying to think of something to write, suggest starting with something familiar. New techniques of "Mind-Mapping," now taught in most schools, help limber up ideas and can provide an organizational guide for the writing. (See *Your Child's Growing Mind*, by Jane M. Healy, Ph.D., Doubleday, Inc., 1994, and consult the Recommended Reading list for suggestions on how to use this important new thinking aid.)

5. **Remember that good writers make many drafts before they are satisfied.** Help your child develop an initial plan (which idea comes first, which next, etc.), but expect her to do some re-writing. Don't ever encourage (or allow) your child to copy text from a book without properly citing the source. Not only is this practice illegal, but it does nothing to teach the child to write independently. If you are unsure of the rules on this issue, check with the teacher.

6. **Don't expect your child to concentrate on content and mechanics all at once.** The brain has different circuits for spelling, punctuation rules and ideas. *Remember, in the long run, the ideas are the most important.*

Troubleshooting

For specific difficulties in spelling and punctuation, some of the newer computer software drill programs can be useful and fun for the child. Find out if any are available from the school, an educational resource facility (ask your school reading specialist) or the library.

The most common problem in writing, however, is not with spelling or punctuation. Rather, it's when a child who has great ideas and can talk intelligently about them lacks the fortitude or skill to get them down on paper. Often this scenario includes some combination of the following: increasingly frequent "loss" of homework papers, failure to bring home assignments on time, outright refusal to complete written work, "messy" papers, bad spelling and handwriting that looks as if a dizzy chicken had strolled backwards across the paper.

Contrary to general belief, a child who exhibits several of these warning signs is not usually lazy or unmotivated. More often, the difficulty stems from a developmental problem with "output," and may also include problems with organization (messy desk, untied shoes). The important things to remember are:

- **Do not accuse the child of laziness or not caring.**

- **If this pattern continues for six months or more, and no other cause can be found (e.g., a crisis at home, physical illness), insist on a special evaluation from the school psychologist—or an outside clinic if necessary.** Many bright children with learning differences first run into trouble in this manner. It is critical to get the child specialized help as soon as possible.

- **If this pattern is long-standing for one of your older children, it's not too late to seek professional help from a learning specialist.** Sometimes even the best schools and teachers fail to understand and treat this type of output problem in a child who is an adequate reader and seems otherwise intelligent.

Helping with Math and Science

New Views for a Technological Age

Math and science represent two solid cornerstones for success in our rapidly evolving technological world. Yet they, too, have changed in educators' views during the past few years. What is math, anyway? Most of us were taught that it is mainly doing calculations on paper following certain rules (or "algorithms") that we have memorized (multiplication tables, order of operations, etc.). What is science? It is memorizing data and long terms, in the experience of many ex-students.

A few parents were lucky enough to have teachers who understood the real reasons for studying math and science: to teach students to be effective reasoners and problem solvers! They will find it easier to help their children in this new era; the rest of us have some mental readjustment ahead.

Memorizing certain rules and procedures is still essential, of course. In math, children need to learn how and why to calculate (add, subtract, multiply, divide) and they need to be exposed to the processes, such as long division, that used to occupy all of math class. Nowadays, however, many schools encourage the use of hand-held calculators, so that class time can be shifted from pure calculation to more advanced uses of mathematics: graphing, statistics, probability and the like (terms and concepts that many parents were never even exposed to unless they majored in math in college). Children in a computer/calculator age must understand not only how to solve math problems, but also why, so they'll know what information to feed into the machines and how to interpret it intelligently when it comes out.

Likewise in science classes, students may now be working with computer simulations of experiments, or communicating on electronic bulletin boards with real scientists conducting real experiments in any part of the world. Such "hands-on" interaction with important scientific concepts and procedures produces much better learning and memory—and a lot of enthusiasm for studying science!

"Hands-on" interaction with important scientific concepts and procedures produces much better learning and memory—and a lot of enthusiasm for studying science!

Many classes for elementary and middle school students also make use of "manipulatives": blocks, cubes, rods, brightly-colored graphs and other real-life objects that teach the basic concepts in a manner interesting and appropriate for the age group. Wise parents encourage the use of these proven aids to concept mastery.

These developments tend to leave some of us a bit breathless, but it's important that we encourage our schools to adopt the best of the new, while considering carefully what is worthwhile keeping from the past. Here are some fundamental skills for math and science success:

- Curiosity and flexibility in thinking

- Ability to make calculated guesses (estimation and hypothesis formation)

- Ability to develop and follow a logical train of thought

- Understanding of cause and effect ("If I build the block tower too high, it will fall over." "If I spend all my allowance on a CD, I won't have enough for lunch money.")

- Ability to categorize and classify (All triangles have three sides. Animals, birds and reptiles belong to different categories.)

- Ability to stick to a problem even if it looks hard and doesn't come easily on the first try

Whatever happened to simple counting? Understanding numerical relationships is important, of course, but we now realize that simply memorizing is not enough. Don't let your child be like one little boy who came home from first grade. When his mother asked him what he had learned in school, he replied, "I learned that three plus four is seven. Mom, what's seven?" Our children need real-life experiences with quantity and number to show them what the numerals (the written "numbers") really mean. Older students also need to see math and science "in action," perhaps by visiting job sites or talking with workers who use these skills every day. Take every opportunity to expose your children to people and situations that can reinforce the importance of math and science.

Our children need real-life experiences with quantity and number to show them what the numerals (the written "numbers") really mean.

Building a Strong Math/Science Foundation

First, help children of any age become good problem solvers. Here are some tips:

1. **Encourage questions,** particularly those which have more than one possible answer, and preferably ones to which *you* don't know the answer. ("I'm not sure why leaves have different shapes—let's collect some and try to figure out some reasons.")

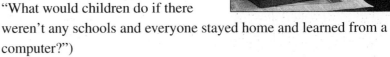

2. **Ask open-ended questions and welcome innovative responses.** ("What do you think these woods will look like a hundred years from now?" "What would children do if there weren't any schools and everyone stayed home and learned from a computer?")

3. **Encourage divergent approaches to everyday situations, within reason.** (If your child can think of a reason for setting the table in a new and different way, why not?)

4. **Help your child to tolerate some uncertainty**—effective thinkers can delay the best solution to a problem until they have tried out several hypotheses.

5. **Provide toys and games that encourage a variety of types of play which the youngster must create himself;** praise and admire innovative uses of play construction, or game materials.

6. **Show your child how to estimate.** ("You have nine pennies in your bank—that's close to a dime." "We have to drive 295 miles to Grandmother's house—that's almost 300 miles.")

7. **Practice "guess and test."** ("I'm not sure what will happen if we put lemonade in the Jell-O instead of water—let's guess some possibilities and then see what happens.")

8. **Avoid using the words "right" and "wrong" unless a moral or safety issue is at stake; take time to listen to the child's ideas before passing judgment.** Try out the phrase "That's an interesting idea—tell me more."

9. **Work hard on helping your child feel secure enough to take sensible risks.**

(Material in "Building a Strong Math/Science Foundation" from *Your Child's Growing Mind*, by Jane M. Healy, Ph.D., Doubleday, Inc. 1994.)

Practical Learning

Next, try some family activities to build numerical and scientific concepts:

- **Cooking** offers a wealth of possibilities for understanding the important ideas of quantity, measuring, sequencing steps in a problem, following directions accurately, fractions and testing hypotheses. Here is an enjoyable, meaningful and delicious learning experience!

- **Family games** involving cards, numbers or money promote an understanding of relative quantity and build computational skills.

Games requiring visual organization or strategy are also valuable.

- **Shopping** offers chances to compare prices, shapes, learn about decimal places and practice computation in a meaningful situation. Catalogue shopping at home can become a math game—figuring out how many items can be purchased for a certain amount, for example.

- Every school-age child should have some sort of **allowance** to manage, however small, and real experience buying small items and getting change. Older children can learn about interest in a natural context from a bank or if they need to borrow from the parental exchequer.

- **Travel games**, such as license plate bingo, keeping mileage records or even computing gas mileage can be fun. Working with maps builds graphing and directional skills and can make a child feel very important.

- **Collecting** inspires many budding scientists, and **exploring nature** with an interested adult has kindled the interest of many future biologists.

- **Measuring and weighing** activities are appropriate even for young children. Making diagrams of rooms in the house or maps of the yard or neighborhood is fun. You might try introducing nonstandard measurements, such as "How many Daddy-shoe-lengths wide is the kitchen?" The *Guinness Book of World Records* is a rich source of relative measurements.

- **Using time** is the best way to learn about it. Relate time to events that are meaningful for the child and use appropriate terms ("What are we doing *now*?"; "What will we do *after/while* we eat lunch?"). Pasting or drawing pictures of activities on a daily calendar while discussing past and upcoming events makes "then" and "soon" more understandable than using abstract concepts of days, weeks, months or seasons.

- **Following directions** is one of the most important skills from the home. Taking steps in order, planning ahead and talking about what to do before tackling the task can all be encouraged. Cooking, as noted earlier, treasure hunts and building models are all sequential step-following activities. For older children, map and compass skills are very helpful.

- **Calculator games** are a good source of problem-solving situations with numerical concepts.

These are only a few of the multitude of activities which are the natural base of math and science learning. They are essentially about the real world, which is the best place to learn about them.

(Material in "Practical Learning" from *Your Child's Growing Mind,* by Jane M. Healy, Ph.D., Doubleday, Inc. 1994.)

Troubleshooting

1. **Watch for multiple danger signs (listed below) that persist for several months.** Many students experience temporary "glitches" in the learning process, so exercise reasonable patience and help the child try to work the problem out. (For younger children, you may need to take action more promptly than for older ones.) Danger signs:

    - 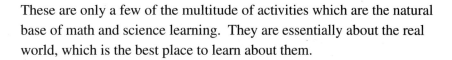 confusion about math or science homework

- frequently writing numerals backwards or confusing plus and minus signs after age seven or eight

- tears or stomachaches on test days

- persistent difficulty learning "facts" (addition, subtraction, multiplication tables)

- trouble estimating (gives far-fetched answers to story problems)

2. **Keep a folder of papers that document the child's difficulty.**

3. **Schedule a conference with the teacher.** Discuss the child's papers you have saved. Find out if special help is available at school. If necessary, ask to speak to the school psychologist or learning specialist.

4. **If the school has not been using manipulatives (concrete objects such as blocks, rods or geometric forms that teach number concepts), ask if some trained person could use them to work with your child during free time or after school.** For older students, teachers usually offer extra help periods. Expect your child to sign up (and show up) for any extra help that is offered.

5. **If outside help is your only recourse, look for a clinic or experienced tutor who will use many different approaches other than worksheets to get the concepts across.**

An Important Postscript for Parents of Girls

Many potentially talented female mathematicians, engineers or scientists have been deterred by a culture that says "Girls aren't supposed to be good at those things." Studies show that parents' (and teachers') attitudes have a lot to do with this loss of talent and personal accomplishment. Please encourage your daughters to feel curiosity and a sense of satisfaction in tackling more technical subjects—not just by churning out "perfect" papers of sums, but by taking some intellectual risks: "What would happen if . . . ?"; "How could that be different . . . ?"; "What do you guess will happen . . . ?" Expect as much of her as you would of a boy. She will surprise you!

Enjoy!

Parents who follow the ideas in this chapter and this book have many delightful experiences ahead—and inevitably, some frustrating ones as well! We can give you one guarantee: You won't do a perfect job, but you will experience the satisfaction of working, learning and growing with your child as you observe the amazing process of mental development in action.

EVALUATE THE COACH

Using the suggestions in Chapter 6, choose an activity in which you coach your child's learning. For example, you could choose spending time reading with your child. Afterwards, evaluate your own performance with the following checklist.

Tips   **Evaluation (E = Excellent;
                                             S = Satisfactory;
                                             N = Needs improvement)**

1. I am available to my child.   _____

2. I offer support, not criticism.   _____

3. I focus on effort and improvement
    instead of grades.   _____

4. I don't worry about being an expert.   _____

5. I don't expect perfection.   _____

6. I turn the thinking over to my child.   _____

7. I enjoy coaching my child.   _____

What will you do to improve your coaching next time?   _____

_____

_____

_____

CREATIVE LEARNING OPPORTUNITIES

One of the ideas stressed in Chapter 8 is that learning opportunities can be found in every-day activities, from math games to trips to a museum. Build your own collection of favorite learning activities by trying new ones with your children and then record the results.

Activity	Child	Evaluation (E=excellent; S=satisfactory; N=needs improvement)

1. _____ _____ _____

    I can improve this activity by: _____

    _____

2. _____ _____ _____

    I can improve this activity by: _____

    _____

3. _____ _____ _____

    I can improve this activity by: _____

    _____

4. _____ _____ _____

    I can improve this activity by: _____

    _____

5. _____ _____ _____

    I can improve this activity by: _____

    _____

Activity	Child	Evaluation (E=excellent; S=satisfactory; N=needs improvement)

6. _____ _____ _____

  I can improve this activity by: _____

  _____

7. _____ _____ _____

  I can improve this activity by: _____

  _____

8. _____ _____ _____

  I can improve this activity by: _____

  _____

9. _____ _____ _____

  I can improve this activity by: _____

  _____

10. _____ _____ _____

  I can improve this activity by: _____

  _____

11. _____ _____ _____

  I can improve this activity by: _____

  _____

HOMES FOR GOOD READERS

Here's a quick summary of research on home environments that give youngsters a boost in reading.

- A nonpunitive but structured atmosphere where children are encouraged to express ideas and feel part of decision making.

- Absence of unrealistic restrictions, demands or inappropriate pressure.

- Encouragement of independent problem solving. Preschoolers are encouraged to be self-reliant in zipping, tying, setting table, etc. Older children are expected to think through problems.

- Tolerance of reasonable mistakes.

- Focus on praise rather than criticism.

- Emphasis on expanding rather than correcting child's conversation.

- No forcing of early reading.

- Adult models of reading for a variety of purposes. Pleasure in reading is evident. Boys and girls see both parents reading, since children tend to copy the attitudes of the same-sex parent.

■ Regular time for reading to the child; reading is associated with relaxed and loving contact.

■ Availability of books, newspapers, magazines and interesting children's books; TV time regulated.

■ Regular trips to the library, where the child is encouraged to select books that are personally meaningful.

■ A broad range of experiences, and conversation about them, is a regular part of family life.

(Material in "Homes for Good Readers" from *Your Child's Growing Mind*, by Jane M. Healy, Ph.D., Doubleday, Inc. 1994.)

20 WAYS TO SUPPORT YOUR CHILDREN AND THEIR SCHOOL

Parents have asked how they can support their children's teachers in doing the best job they can for their students. Here are 20 helpful ways that you can show your support.

1. **Talk positively about the school experience.** Even if your own school memories were not always pleasant, you can help your child by emphasizing the positive opportunity that school affords him. Rather than "You have to go to school today," you might try "You get to go to school today."

2. **Talk positively about teachers, education and homework.** Your positive attitude can help your child develop a positive approach to school.

3. **Show interest in what your child is learning.** By asking questions and letting your child share, you communicate that learning is important and stimulating. Again, emphasize the positive. Rather than ask the standard "What did you do in school, today?"; try some variations, such as, "What did you do that you really liked?"; "What did you feel good about?"; "What would you like to learn more about?"; "What are you reading?"

4. **Continue learning.** Your child sees you as a model for many things. If you continue to expand your own knowledge and skills by reading or perhaps even taking a course, your child sees the value in learning.

5. **Let your child teach you.** As someone once said, "To teach is to learn twice." You can strengthen your child's learning by letting her explain new concepts to you.

6. **Help your child find ways to apply his learning to everyday life.** The more practical information seems to be, the more motivated your child will be to tackle new material.

7. **Avoid the grade trap.** While grades are useful in assessing how much your child is learning, it is the learning, not the grades, that is our goal. Avoid the trap of making grades a competition. Help your child learn to relax and enjoy learning without the pressure to compete.

8. **Avoid comparing your child's grades with others.** Such comparisons are almost always discouraging and counterproductive. It is much better to compare your child's grades with her own grades from the previous report card. "Where have you improved?" "Where do you want to improve more?" "How will you accomplish this?" "How can I help?"

9. **Develop realistic expectations for your child.** Encourage your child to do the best he can in school, keeping in mind that children will naturally do better in some areas than in others. Also keep in mind that your child is special because of who he is, not how he performs.

10. **Provide a quiet place and time for homework.** Most students do best with a regular study time that they have agreed upon with their parents. Having a special place for homework, whether it's a quiet desk in their own rooms or at the kitchen table, helps build a routine and atmosphere conducive to work. This can't be accomplished in front of the TV.

11. **Go over your child's work with her.** Going over homework and papers sent home with an interest in what your child is doing gives you an opportunity to encourage her work and to notice if she is having trouble.

12. **Be a homework consultant, not a tutor.** Homework is your child's work, not yours. We recommend that you not sit by your child in an attempt to make sure everything is answered correctly. Mistakes on homework are one way your child's teacher learns what concepts need more explanation. Instead, act as a consultant, being available to offer support and help when your child asks.

13. **Encourage your child to read at home.** Since reading is the cornerstone of much learning, the more your child practices this essential skill, the better he will do in all his subjects. To maintain the motivation and enjoyment of reading, let your child choose what he wants to read. Easy books, magazines, even comic books as a last resort—anything but material that's "not for children"— should be encouraged.

14. **Develop a consistent and effective discipline plan.** Using parenting methods that teach your child responsibility, cooperation and self-esteem will also help your child do well in the classroom. You can avoid being too strict or too lax by taking a parent education course or reading some of the recommended books.

15. **Support the school's discipline plan.** A school, like a family, must maintain a certain level of order and structure so that all our children can feel safe and able to learn. If your child is disciplined at school, please help your child learn from the experience by backing up the school at home. If you have a problem with the plan, please bring it up with the administration.

16. **Check out disturbing reports.** Teachers, as well as parents and students, are not perfect. They may make mistakes. However, if your child shares with you something her teacher did that she felt was grossly unfair or unkind, listen respectfully but don't assume it was as bad as it sounds. Children sometimes exaggerate when their feelings are hurt. If you are disturbed about a situation, call the teacher and check it out. A concerned tone of voice, rather than a hostile or angry tone, will help.

17. **Bring a solution as well as a problem.** If you have a concern or see a problem you think needs correcting and you bring it to the attention of your child's teacher, also bring a supportive attitude and an idea for a solution. This will help build a cooperative, problem-solving relationship.

18. **Be careful about misinformation and gossip.** The school "grapevine" can produce a lot of useful information, but it can also become a version of the old game "telephone," where messages become more and more distorted. You can show your support by checking out such information with your child's teacher or the administration. Please call ahead to set up a meeting rather than dropping by for a "quick conference." Your concerns are important to the school and deserve not to be rushed.

19. **Come to class meetings when you are invited.** These meetings not only provide you with important information, but your attendance also communicates to your child that he and the school are important.

20. **Let the school know what is going on at home.** When families go through extra stress such as an illness, a death or a divorce, it can affect the children the most. Please let your child's teacher know about such circumstances. She can often help. In addition, informing the teacher will alert her to possible changes in your child's behavior. (See *A Stress Management Guide for Young People*, by Bettie B. Youngs, Ph.D., Ed.D., Jalmar Press, 1992, for more information on children and stress.)

(Material in "20 Ways to Support Your Children and Their School" from *Active Teaching*, by Michael H. Popkin, Ph.D., Active Parenting Publishers, 1994.)

RECOMMENDED READING LIST

Books

Albert, Linda, and Michael H. Popkin. *Quality Parenting.* New York: Random House, 1987.

Amabile, Theresa. *Growing Up Creative.* New York: Creative Education Foundation, 1992.

Armstrong, Thomas. *In Their Own Way: Discovering and Encouraging Your Child's Personal Learning Style.* Los Angeles: Jeremy Tarcher, 1987.

Coloroso, Barbara. *Kids Are Worth It!: Giving Your Child the Gift of Inner Discipline.* New York: William Morrow and Company, Inc., 1994.

Conners, Keith. *Feeding the Brain.* New York: Plenum Press, 1989.

deBono, Edward. *Teach Your Child How to Think.* New York: Penguin Books, 1993.

Drydon, Gordon, and Jeanette Vos. *The Learning Revolution.* Rolling Hills Estates, Calif.: Jalmar Press, 1984.

Elkind, David. *The Hurried Child.* Rev. ed. Reading, Mass.: Addison-Wesley Publishing Company, 1991.

Gardner, Howard. *Multiple Intelligences: The Theory in Practice.* New York: Basic Books, 1993.

Hallowell, Edward M., and John J. Ratey. *Driven to Distraction: Recognizing and Coping with Attention Deficit Disorder from Childhood through Adulthood.* New York: Pantheon Books, 1994.

Hartmann, Thom. *Attention Deficit Disorder: A Different Perception.* Penn Valley, Calif.: Underwood-Miller, 1993.

Healy, Jane M. *Endangered Minds: Why Children Don't Think and What We Can Do about It.* New York: Simon & Schuster (Touchstone), 1991.

————. *How to Have Intelligent and Creative Conversations with Your Kids.* New York: Doubleday, Inc., 1994.

————. *Your Child's Growing Mind: A Practical Guide to Brain Development and Learning from Birth to Adolescence.* Rev. ed. New York: Doubleday, Inc., 1994.

Ingersoll, Barbara, Ph.D. *Your Hyperactive Child: A Parent's Guide to Coping with Attention Deficit Disorder.* New York: Doubleday, 1988.

Kanter, Patsy F. *Helping Your Child Learn Math.* U.S. Government Printing Office, 1992.

Levine, Melvin *Keeping a Head in School.* Cambridge, Mass.: Educators Publishing Service, Inc., 1990.

Popkin, Michael H. *Active Parenting: Teaching Cooperation, Courage and Responsibility.* New York: HarperCollins, 1987.

————. *Active Parenting Today Parent's Guide.* Atlanta, Ga.: Active Parenting Publishers, 1993.

————. *Active Parenting of Teens Parent's Guide.* Marietta, Ga.: Active Parenting Publishers, 1990.

Ripple, Richard E., Robert R. Biehler, and Gail A. Jaquish. *Human Development.* Boston, Mass.: Houghton Mifflin Co., 1983.

Tonges, Marian J., and Miles V. Zints. *Teaching Reading, Thinking, Study Skills in Content Classrooms.* 2nd ed. Dubuque, Iowa: William C. Brown, 1987.

Vail, Priscilla. *Smart Kids with Social Problems.* New York: NAL, 1989.

Vail, Priscilla. *Learning Styles.* Rosemont, N.J.: Modern Learning Press, 1992.

Wycoff, Joyce. *Mindmapping: Your Personal Guide to Exploring Creativity and Problem Solving.* New York: Berkley Books, 1991.

Youngs, Bettie B. *A Stress Management Guide for Young People.* Rolling Hills Estates, Calif.: Jalmar Press, 1994.

———. *Developing Self-Esteem in Your Students (A K-12 Curriculum Guide).* Rolling Hills Estates, Calif.: Jalmar Press, 1992.

———. *Friendship Is Forever, Isn't It?* Rolling Hills Estates, Calif.: Jalmar Press, 1992.

———. *Goal Setting Skills for Young People.* Rolling Hills Estates, Calif.: Jalmar Press, 1992.

———. *How to Develop Self-Esteem in Your Child: 6 Vital Ingredients.* New York: Fawcett, 1993.

———. *Keeping Your Children Safe: A Parent's Guide to Physical, Emotional, Spiritual and Intellectual Wellness.* San Diego: Learning Tools, 1993.

———. *Problem Solving Skills for Children.* Rolling Hills Estates, Calif.: Jalmar Press, 1992.

———. *Safeguarding Your Teenager From the Dragons of Life: A Guide to the Adolescent Years.* Deerfield Beach, Fla.: Health Communications, 1993.

———. *Self-Esteem and the Educator: It's Job Criteria #1.* Rolling Hills Estates, Calif.: Jalmar Press, 1992.

————. *Stress and Your Child: Helping Kids Cope with the Strains and Pressures of Life.* New York: Random House, 1995.

————. *Values from the Heartland.* Deerfield Beach, Fla.: Health Communications, 1995.

————. *You & Self-Esteem: A Book for Young People (Grades 5-12).* Rolling Hills Estates, Calif.: Jalmar Press, 1992.

BIBLIOGRAPHY

Books

Adams, Marilyn J. *Beginning to Read.* Cambridge, Mass.: MIT Press, 1994.

Baker, Susan. *Parents' Guide to Nutrition.* Reading, Mass.: Addison-Wesley Publishing Co., Inc., 1986.

Ban, John R. *Parents Assuring Student Success (PASS): Achievement Made Easy by Learning Together.* Bloomington, Ill.: National Education Service, 1993.

Bell, Nanci. *Visualizing and Verbalizing.* Rev. ed. Paso Robels, Calif.: Academy of Reading Publications, 1991.

Boggiano, Ann K., and Thanes Pittman, ed. *Achievement and Motivation.* New York: Cambridge University Press, 1992.

Center for National Origin, Race and Sex Equity. *The Fourth R: Responsibility.* Portland, Ore.: Northwest Regional Educational Laboratory, 1988.

Cooper, Kenneth H. *Kid Fitness.* New York: Bantam Books, 1991.

Fuller, Cheri. *Homelife—The Key to Your Child's Success at School.* Tulsa, Okla.: Honor Books, 1988.

————. *Motivating Your Kids from Crayons to Career.* Tulsa, Okla.: Honor Books, 1990.

Gibson, K. R., and A. C. Peterson, ed. *Brain Maturation and Cognitive Development.* New York: Aldine de Gruyter, 1991.

Gilbert, Sara. *How to Take Tests.* New York: William Morrow and Company, Inc., 1983.

Gruber, Gary. *Dr. Gruber's Essential Guide to Test Taking for Kids.* New York: William Morrow and Company, Inc., 1986.

Healy, Jane M. *Endangered Minds: Why Children Don't Think and What We Can Do about It.* New York: Simon & Schuster (Touchstone), 1991.

———. *How to Have Intelligent and Creative Conversations with Your Kids.* New York: Doubleday, Inc., 1994.

———. *Your Child's Growing Mind: A Practical Guide to Brain Development and Learning from Birth to Adolescence.* Rev. ed. New York: Doubleday, Inc., 1994.

Henderson, Anne T., and Nancy Berla. *The Family is Critical to Student Achievement.* National Committee for Citizens in Education, 1994.

Moloney, Kathleen. *Parent's Guide to Feeding Your Kids Right.* New York: Prentice Hall Press, 1989.

Ohio University Southern Campus. *Together We Can Parent Handbook.* Irinton, Ohio: Ohio University Southern Campus, 1990.

Ohio University Southern Campus. *Together We Can Facilitator Handbook.* Irinton, Ohio: Ohio University Southern Campus, 1990.

Pennington, Bruce F. *Diagnosing Learning Disorders: A Neuropsychological Framework.* New York: Guilford Press, 1991.

Popkin, Michael H. *Active Parenting: Teaching Cooperation, Courage and Responsibility.* New York: HarperCollins, 1987.

———. *Active Parenting Today Parent's Guide.* Atlanta, Ga.: Active Parenting Publishers, 1993.

———. *Active Parenting of Teens Parent's Guide.* Marietta, Ga.: Active Parenting Publishers, 1990.

———. *Active Teaching Teacher's Handbook.* Atlanta, Ga.: Active Parenting Publishers, Inc., 1994

Trieman, Rebecca. *Learning to Spell.* New York: Oxford Press, 1993.

Youngs Bettie B. *Developing Self-Esteem in Your Students (A K-12 Curriculum Guide).* Rolling Hills Estates, Calif.: Jalmar Press, 1992.

———. *How to Develop Self-Esteem in Your Child: 6 Vital Ingredients.* New York: Fawcett, 1993.

————. *Keeping Your Children Safe: A Parent's Guide to Physical, Emotional, Spiritual and Intellectual Wellness.* San Diego: Learning Tools, 1993.

————. *Problem Solving Skills for Children.* Rolling Hills Estates, Calif.: Jalmar Press, 1992.

————. *Safeguarding Your Teenager From the Dragons of Life: A Guide to the Adolescent Years.* Deerfield Beach, Fla.: Health Communications, 1993.

————. *Self-Esteem and the Educator: It's Job Criteria #1.* Rolling Hills Estates, Calif.: Jalmar Press, 1992.

————. *Values from the Heartland.* Deerfield Beach, Fla.: Health Communications, 1995.

————. *You & Self-Esteem: A Book for Young People (Grades 5-12).* Rolling Hills Estates, Calif.: Jalmar Press, 1992.

Articles

Brophy, Jere. "Synthesis of Research on Strategies for Motivating Students to Learn." *Educational Leadership* 45, no. 2 (1987): 40–48.

Grolnick, Wendy, and Richard Ryan. "Parent Styles Associated with Children's Self-Regulation and Competence in School." *Journal of Educational Psychology* 81, no. 2 (1989): 143–154.

Health Watch. *Aging*, no. 366 (1994): 2–13

Matarazzo, Joseph D. "Psychological Testing and Assessment in the 21st Century." *American Psychologist* 47, no. 8 (1992): 1007–1018.

Pintrich, Paul R. "Current Issues and New Directions in Motivational Theory and Research: Special Issue" *Educational Psychologist* 26 (1991): 3–4.

Spector, Janet. "Predicting Progress in Beginning Reading: Dynamic Assessment of Phonemic Awareness." *Journal of Educational Psychology* 84, no. 3 (1992): 353–363.

Sternberg, Robert J. "Ability Tests, Measurements, and Markets." *Journal of Educational Psychology* 84, no. 2 (1992): 134–140.